Walking Through the Storm: A Story of Recovery from Sex Addiction

Walking Through the Storm: A Story of Recovery from Sex Addiction

Brady C

© 2018 Brady C
All rights reserved.

ISBN-13: 9781983451355
ISBN-10: 1983451355

To those men and women still caught in the web of sex addiction, I have written this book for you, your families, and others seeking a better understanding of the disease of sex addiction. Recovery is possible.

Table of Contents

Introduction · ix

What It Was Like · 1
Chapter 1   The Conundrum · 3
Chapter 2   Memories · 5
Chapter 3   Life on the Playground · · · · · · · · · · · · · · · · · · · 9
Chapter 3   Life at Home ·13
Chapter 4   Success ·16
Chapter 5   Trauma ·18
Chapter 6   Wings · 22
Chapter 7   Where Am I Going? ·27
Chapter 8   A Seemingly Unimportant Decision · · · · · · · · · ·32
Chapter 9   Time to Move On ·35
Chapter 10 Another Seemingly Unimportant Decision · · · · · · · 42
Chapter 11 The Last Big Move – Sort Of · · · · · · · · · · · · · · ·52
Chapter 12 Pornography · 54

What Happened · 59
Chapter 13 Caught ·61
Chapter 14 Into Treatment ·74
Chapter 15 Understanding Sexual Addiction · · · · · · · · · · · · 80
Chapter 16 You Too? I Thought I Was the Only One. · · · · · · · · ·87
Chapter 17 I'm Not Much, But I'm All I Think About · · · · · · · ·95

Chapter 18 Family Therapy · 99
Chapter 19 Learning About Recovery · 109
Chapter 20 Humility · 115
Chapter 21 Sentencing · 120
Chapter 22 Prison · 123
Chapter 23 Separation · 128
Chapter 24 Finally Someone to Talk to Inside · · · · · · · · · · · · · · 131
Chapter 25 Recovery and the Twelve Steps · · · · · · · · · · · · · · · · 139
Chapter 26 Going Home · 152

What It's Like Now · **161**
Chapter 27 Spirituality · 163

Appendix 1 – Does Treatment Work? · · · · · · · · · · · · · · · · · 171
Appendix 2 – Pornography: A Public Health Issue · · · · · · · 175
Appendix 3 – The Science of Sexual Addiction · · · · · · · · · 179
Appendix 4 – Reflections on Society: Overreaction,
Injustice, and Rehabilitation · 183
Appendix 5 – Twelve Step Resources for Sex Addiction
and Codependence · 201
Acknowledgements · 203
Endnotes · 205
About the Author · 217

Introduction

"Mr. C., I don't want you to die in prison. But you might."

--A Federal Judge

As a person many looked up to and even envied, I had what appeared to be a successful thirty-five-year marriage to my wife Ellyn, three thriving children, and a high-profile career. What was hidden from others was the fact that for most of my life I had been leading two lives, and the values of those lives were direct opposites to each other.

A nationally known public speaker with an Ivy League education, for much of my adult life I traveled the country, speaking and writing on the values of leading a moral life. I was a religious man, considered by many to be an expert on ethics, integrity, honor, and citizenship, and was thought to be a man who practiced those virtues. I held those values dear then, and still do.

But the truth of my double life came crashing down on me and those who had trusted me early one morning in March 2004, when a dozen armed federal officers pounded on my front door, demanding to be let into our home. They had a search warrant. Ellyn was confused and terrified. I knew why they were there. My name is Brady and I'm a sex addict. This is my story.

For almost seven years I had been viewing pornography on the Internet. Some of those images were hidden on my home computer, including degrading pictures of children engaged in sexual activity. I had received those images by email from others, and I had sent them to those who wanted them. I spent hours every day on the computer, away from my wife and family, depriving them of time they deserved from me. Most importantly, I pulled away from God, my ethical system, and my personal moral code. I knew what I was doing was wrong, but I could not stop.

There is general acceptance that drugs and alcohol are addictive to some people. There is less agreement on whether behaviors can be equally addictive. When does a passion for sex and pornography or a passion for gambling become an addiction? To me addiction is a pattern of thoughts, feelings, and actions that are damaging to self and others, which becomes progressively worse over time, and which the individual is unable to stop even though he knows the consequences. That's what happened to me. Again, I knew I had a problem. I spent an increasing amount of time looking at pornography. The pornography I sought became progressively more deviant.

Eventually my addiction reached out beyond the pornography and I began engaging in sexual activity outside my marriage. I engaged in sexual activity with strangers, people I did not know or care about, adults I met online or in hotels, in video stores, or in bars or clubs. Again, I knew what I was doing was wrong. And yet, for reasons at the time totally beyond my understanding, I could not stop.

Addicts stop when the pain of the addiction becomes greater than the pain of stopping. I stopped on the day federal agents came to my house with a search warrant.

The consequences of my behavior were severe: damaged relationships, loss of job. I had no confidence that the time in prison I knew was coming would relieve my desire to act out sexually, so three months after my arrest I checked into one of the premier facilities in the country for the treatment of addictions, including sex addiction. I remained there for over four months, learning about those things that influenced me to act as I had acted and discovering how to begin recovering from sex addiction. The decision to undertake residential treatment for sex addiction is the most important decision I have ever made.

In treatment I was introduced to the programs of several twelve-step groups and learned that addicts who are committed to getting better, to recover from their disease, can successfully help each other. I faced the truth of my behavior and stopped lying. I became reacquainted with God. I began to recover.

The sentencing process in Federal courts begins with an investigation and report from the probation department. My attorney said this would be the worst part of the legal process, and it was. The probation department investigated the details of my criminal behavior, my personal background, and my finances. They then used a numerical formula from the "Federal Sentencing Guidelines" to recommend a sentence to the judge. The probation department recommended that I be sentenced to a term of 17 ½ to 20 years in Federal prison.

Prior to sentencing the judge received over 130 letters from friends and family attesting to my otherwise good character. I was a first-time offender. Even with the damaging presentence report, I had hopes of a light sentence.

But on April 27, 2005, that hope disappeared. The judge had delayed my sentencing so that I could complete treatment. But now, just over 13 months after the police first came to my house looking for evidence, I was in a Federal courtroom, along with my family and a few friends, to learn my sentence for receipt and distribution of child pornography. We made a brief presentation. One member spoke for the family, giving a moving statement. I spoke briefly, admitting guilt and expressing regret. A representative from the treatment center explained sex addiction and my treatment. The judge recessed the court to make a decision. When the recess was extended to thirty minutes, my hopes skyrocketed. Perhaps the judge heard what we said, although he never looked at me once during my presentation. My family and friends were optimistic. Then came the sentence:

"Mr. C., I don't want you to die in prison, but you might."

I felt as if my heart stopped. I could no longer lie to myself. It was going to be bad. "I sentence you to ninety-seven months in Federal prison, and five years of supervised release." In the back of the courtroom, I heard my wife Ellyn scream. I began writing my story.

I'm writing not because my personal story is unique, but because it's not. Too many people end up in a place in their lives where they never intended to go, never believed they could go, and certainly never wanted to go. I'm only one of them.

I served just over seven years in Federal prison and have been home for several years. Hope has reappeared, and I can see the future. The twelve steps of Alcoholics Anonymous[i], which serve as the basis for all twelve-step programs, promise me that "We will not regret the past nor wish to shut the door on it" and "No matter how far down the scale we have gone, we will see how our experience can benefit others.[ii]" Those promises and more are coming true in my life. I hope others can learn from my experience – what sex addiction was like for me, how I became an addict, what I did to recover and maintain recovery, and what my life is like now.

Not many marriages survive a partner with sex addiction. Very few survive long prison sentences. The story of my recovery is quite remarkable, but the story of the growth of Ellyn's and my marriage is even more so. We're pleased to share that story as well. Each recovery from addiction is a personal story, different from any other. We hope the story of our recovery will be valuable to you.

We've chosen to tell our story anonymously. There are two reasons for that. First, the publicity that surrounded my arrest and conviction extracted a considerable toll on my family, my employer, my church, and others around me. I victimized them once by my behavior; I do not wish to do so again. Second, the traditions of twelve-step programs first established by Alcoholics Anonymous caution: "Our relations with the general public should be characterized by personal anonymity[iii]." When I choose to speak directly about the benefits of specific programs to me, I need to do so anonymously. My name and picture have not been included in this manuscript. The names, events, and circumstances included are true, but adjusted to protect the anonymity of the individuals involved.

Welcome to my journey walking through the storm of sex addiction. Join with me to discover that recovery from sex addiction is possible, that relationships can be healed, and that addicts and their loved ones can have hope and a bright future. This story will show you the path.

What It Was Like

CHAPTER 1

The Conundrum

INDIVIDUALS MAKE CHOICES AND THEY must take personal responsibility for those choices. Society must act as if the individual is responsible for what he does; our society could not function well otherwise. But the choices we make are impacted by the influence of the families with whom we grew up, events that surround us, the way we learn to think, the biology of our brain, and genetic factors we inherited. Psychology, biology, neurology, and the society in which we live help make us who we are. I believe God plays His role too. We do not do it alone.

Our fundamental character as individual human beings is constantly evolving and developing, shaped by a variety of forces over which we have no control. My father's thrift was shaped by the Great Depression, my mother's self-centeredness by the Roaring Twenties. My character was shaped by my parents and grandfather, by the Boy Scouts and Sunday school, by childhood sex abuse and the bullying of my peers in the high school locker room, by the genetics with which I was born, by my wife's love and also her depression, and by the successes and failures of my career.

In America, we see illness as something that happens to people, but addiction as something for which the individual is responsible. My intention in this volume is to show that sex addiction is an illness, but like a cigarette smoker with lung cancer, the individual shares responsibility for that illness. He is also responsible for its cure.

Why do some people become addicts and others do not? We don't know for sure. We are complex individuals. Determining the cause of addiction is complicated by the fact that addiction is caused by a combination and interaction of several factors, including genetic predisposition to developing the disease, a likely chemical imbalance in the brain, and a group of developmental, social, and stressful life events that help precipitate the illness. The influence of these varies from person to person. We are not all the same. Each of us grew up in a different environment with different genes, different parents, in different circumstances. We start at different places and have different experiences. If you can't imagine how someone like me could do some of the things I've done, it's because you haven't had the same experiences I've had. As my son Fred said, "If this can happen to my dad, it can happen to anybody."

Neurologists, psychologists, and sociologists all have a perspective on the causes of addiction. Twelve step programs and religion add their insight to the mix. No doubt, those who thought they knew me well wondered why I, a leader in my church, an educated person with a successful career, a thirty-five-year marriage, and three wonderful children could descend into dependence on pornography and cross the line into the perversion of child pornography. The truth is: it was as much a mystery to me as it was to them.

I've spent the last ten years studying addiction, particularly sex addiction. I began by doing everything I could to understand my own behavior and recovery, and then looked at others who also found themselves addicted to sex. I've studied the writings of psychologists, sociologists, neuroscientists, theologians, and others. I've attended more than 1,000 twelve-step meetings, and completed court-ordered therapy. With a great deal of help from others, I've rebuilt my relationship with God. I'm going to share my discoveries with you through three voices: my own, those of other sex addicts, and the voices of scientists and other experts. I hope you will find these discoveries as fascinating as I did. I'll begin by sharing the story of my life.

CHAPTER 2

Memories

How does a writer explain his not-so-uncommon life in a way that does not bore the reader into setting down his book in disgust before ever reaching the message? I will attempt to be brief, but not too brief, and describe the elements of my life that seem to have a part in my later fall.

It's unlikely anything will be more important in our lives than the family into which we are born, by sheer genetic luck or the choice of God. My family was white, upper middle class, and American of European stock. Some would have considered it ideal.

The first of the C. family to come to America, Mathias, sailed from England to New Jersey in 1696, but the family stayed in New Jersey only one generation before moving to Canada, where they farmed for the next 100 years. My paternal grandfather, Stanley, immigrated to the United States from Canada and purchased a farm in the Midwest. There he met my grandmother Estelle, whose family, French immigrants, owned a neighboring farm. My grandmother was the youngest of thirteen children, and the only one born in the United States.

Grandpa C. eventually tired of farming and purchased a small company in a Midwestern industrial city, where he and Grandma settled in. They had two children, Bernie and Tom, my father. Grandpa's business was quite successful. He eventually invested in the stock market and became a prominent member of the city's business community. He was active in several of the influential business and social clubs, and became Chairman of the Board of the city's most exclusive country club.

As a child my father, Tom, was a bit of a "hell raiser." Twice he was sent to private boarding schools. Eventually he graduated from a public high school near his home and attended a small university nearby, majoring in engineering. But before Dad graduated, his world took a sudden and unexpected turn that in many ways would dominate the rest of his life, and heavily influence mine. Grandpa had invested extravagantly on margin, borrowing outrageously to purchase more stock as the value of his stock increased. In October 1929 the stock market collapsed, and the price of stocks plunged. Grandpa had borrowed more money than his stock was worth. In a single day Grandpa went from being a millionaire to being broke. His wealth, his prestige, and his hope gone, distraught, my grandfather committed suicide. His business and the family were deeply in debt.

My dad was twenty-two and Uncle Bernie was twenty-eight when they took over a struggling business at the beginning of the Great Depression. Dad was the sales manager; Uncle Bernie managed the operations. Over the next ten years, Dad's life was consumed with paying off bills and keeping the business afloat. By the beginning of World War II, the business was improving, but my father's experience in the Depression colored the way he thought about life.

Dad loved the ladies. One in particular was a pretty redhead, Eleanor, the secretary to the president of a company that was a customer of my dad's. Dad met her on one of his sales calls. Eleanor had graduated from high school when she was only sixteen years old and attended a large state university, majoring in chemistry. Following her sophomore year, Eleanor was looking for a summer job. The company was looking for someone full time. Eleanor lied to get the job, then loved it and stayed. Fifteen years later Dad made a sales call. He got the sale; Eleanor got a husband.

I suspect my mother was as much a playgirl as my father was playboy. She worked part time as a model, and her red hair and green eyes were displayed on billboards around the country. She dated some prominent people, including the coach of a professional football team. Mother danced the Charleston and spoke a lot about speakeasies and Prohibition, although Prohibition was over by the time she met my father.

Mother's parents, Grandpa and Grandma J., moved to this country from Norway around the turn of the century. Eleanor was their only child. Grandpa was a foreman in a manufacturing company. He also remodeled houses. He would buy the house and the family would move in, fix it up while they lived in it, then sell it and buy another one. Grandpa retired when he was fifty-five, and he and Grandma moved to the lake north of the city, where they had vacationed for many years.

My parents' decision to wed was apparently sudden. They eloped, took the train to another state, and got married. On the way to the train, Dad sent a letter to another woman, breaking off what apparently had been a simultaneous relationship. My parents were married six months before the Japanese attacked Pearl Harbor. Dad was thirty-five, mother thirty-four, very old to get married in those days. I came along a year later, the first of three children. I was born into a family with above average affluence and a degree of prominence. My parents were the product of the self-centered Roaring Twenties, the economic turmoil of the thirties, and the war that produced the "Greatest Generation." It should have been a good time to grow up.

World War II was well underway by the time I was born. My parents were living with my Grandmother C. at the time. They knew that Dad was going to be drafted into the Army. He was thirty-six years old, and the Army was getting desperate. They had begun drafting men his age.

After Dad was drafted he went into training. Mother and I followed him where we could, but eventually, following D-Day, he was sent to Europe to fight the Germans. Mother rented a home close to the lake near her retired parents.

My first memory is of my father coming home from World War II. He was in Europe for just over a year, serving as a corporal in the quartermaster corps. He was stationed in Reims, near Eisenhower's headquarters. Dad never talked much about his service in the Army, but he did say that if Eisenhower himself had told him the quickest way home, it wouldn't have been any faster than the way he chose. He volunteered for service in the Pacific, in return for a promised thirty-day furlough at home on the way. Dad guessed that the war would be over before he was sent to the Pacific, and he was right. He arrived at our temporary residence on a joyful evening in early 1946. My first memory is showing him a deck of cards, explaining proudly, "This is the king; this is the jack." I was three years old.

My second memory is not as joyful, although at the time it seemed like just another day. We moved back to the city where my father and uncle worked. We lived in a co-op apartment in a nice section of the city. A small park was located on adjoining land. Even at age four, it was considered safe for me to go to the park alone. It was like playing in my own yard.

One day when I was playing in the park, enjoying some free time, a young man, a stranger to me, asked me to go with him into the woods that adjoined the park. He was an adult, and I was just four years old. Intrigued, I went with him. He asked me to pull down my pants and show him my penis. I did. I have no memory of being afraid or embarrassed. He was an adult, I was a child. I did what the adult asked. I was too young to comprehend the impropriety of his request. He told me if I would come back tomorrow, he would give me a candy bar.

I went home. My mother was standing in the doorway of our apartment, talking to a neighbor. Excited about the prospects of a candy bar, I told her what had happened. I became confused as she hustled me inside. Did my parents call the police? I think so. But like most events of emotional consequence in our family, the event was never mentioned again. A few months later we moved to the suburbs.

Why is it that I remember that experience as clearly today as if it was yesterday? The man did not touch me; there was no physical contact at all. I've received hundreds of Christmas gifts that are long forgotten. Yet, sixty years later, I remember a man who asked me to show him my penis and promised me a candy bar I never received.

A child's perspective is skewed by the limits of a child's perceptions. It was only years later, as an adult, that I began to understand that his behavior was perverted and damaging. Today, in recovery myself, I prefer to see him as a sick man who needed help.

I believe that experience was the first lesson I received that it was acceptable for others to violate my boundaries, which arguably led, years later, to my not respecting the boundaries of the children whose pictures I viewed.

CHAPTER 3

Life on the Playground

WHAT COULD BE MORE AMERICAN in the years after World War II than a move to the suburbs? I spent my childhood in the age of baseball, movies, Cub Scouts, church, and school. It was also an age when my family became less perfect and I began to invisibly learn the traits of an addict.

Our first home in the suburbs was in a small growing town with a population of about 1,400. I was a small child with few friends. Our next-door neighbors had a television, the first one in our neighborhood. Their son was a few years older than I was, but the television was an attraction for children of any age. We spent afternoons watching *Howdy Doody* and *Hopalong Cassidy* in black and white. After a few months other parents decided to recapture their children the only possible way; each family got their own television. Ours was a Philco with a round, thirteen-inch screen. We thought we had entered the modern world.

Our town had a movie theater, with double features on Saturday afternoons and cartoons in between. The theater was six or eight blocks from home. The dirt trail went under the railroad tracks, beneath the viaduct where the trolls lived. I never personally saw any trolls, but they were vividly described by the older boys in the neighborhood. We younger guys were brave and ran under the viaduct anyway.

More important than the theater was the candy shop next door. Baseball cards were just beginning to come back in the early 1950s after being declared nonessential during World War II. For five cents I could get a pack of cards and a piece of bubble gum. Of course, I hoped for cards of my favorite players.

My dad was a lifelong baseball fan, having grown up not far from the field where our city's team played. In his day baseball was played in the daytime, and Dad would go to the field after school to catch the end of the game. When I was growing up, Dad would watch the games on TV on the weekends. He would lie on the family room couch and watch the first inning, then fall asleep. He never failed to wake up by the ninth inning to watch the end of the game. I fondly remember the summer days when he would drop me off at the field to see the game. He was always waiting outside the field when the game ended.

The first time I went to a game by myself was an exciting time. I was eight or nine years old and took the train, the bus, and the streetcar. I could follow the directions today; the streetcar is long gone, but the memories aren't. When the game was over, Dad was there to bring me home. The times have changed; I can't imagine parents putting an eight- or nine-year-old child on the train into a major city without adult supervision today.

Although Dad loved watching baseball, I have no memory of us ever playing catch. Nor did we throw a football or do the other sports-related things boys do with their fathers. I was not a very social child, being asthmatic and not very athletic; I was a frail boy who broke both arms, one falling out of a tree and the other rolling down a dirt hill at a construction site. So I developed hobbies I could do by myself. I loved to read, and read from a very young age: The Bible from cover to cover, history and biographies, fiction, adventure, and books on sports. What I didn't do was make friends easily or succeed playing active outdoor competitive games.

I enjoyed baseball, to watch, not to play. I tried Little League and could hit the ball acceptably, but was terrible in the field. I was afraid of the ball. I began collecting baseball cards when I was about nine. I loved the history of the game and knew every player's batting average, home run totals, and runs batted in. Dreaming the impossible dream of becoming a professional athlete, I isolated and fantasized, developing games I could play by myself and creating teams of my favorite players. Unlike on the field, my team was always pretty good on my bedroom floor. This was my first experience living two lives: the real life as a bright boy with no athletic or social skills, and a fantasy life, isolated with my impossible dreams.

Children or their parents choose to put themselves in an environment that encourages morality and the development of positive friendships, like the church or Scouts. Every Sunday my parents dropped me off at church for Sunday school. I was proud of my five-year perfect attendance pin. I developed friendships at church and was accepted there. Socially, church was a comfortable place for me to be. I learned about God; I did not get to know God.

At home Mother taught me to pray "Now I lay me down to sleep" and "Bless this food…" but I don't remember my parents going to church or acknowledging God as part of our daily life. My parents tried to do the right thing for their children, perhaps not recognizing the message they were sending by their own lack of religious participation.

I joined Cub Scouts when I entered third grade, the beginning of a positive adventure that carried me though high school. We earned Wolf, Bear, and Lion badges, and arrow points for each of the ten achievements from the various Cub Scout books. This was something at which I could excel, and I participated with enthusiasm. I did not have to compete with anyone, as earning the badges was up to me. I earned so many arrow points that they went down my shirttails. I was a lonely young boy with few friends, struggling to reach out, while building the positive traits of self-identity on the things I could do alone.

I enjoyed school. I loved reading and grappling with math problems, and delighted in just being in the classroom. I remember more than one time when I walked over a mile to school after a heavy snowstorm, only to be disappointed to find school closed because of the weather.

The population boom after World War II was in full blossom. When I was ten years old, my parents decided our town was getting too crowded, and we moved again to a small, rural, upper middle-class suburb with a population of no more than a few hundred people – all white, affluent, and Republican. Property zoning allowed home sales only to white Christians, fitting my mother's bias. I moved away from the few friends I had and started over.

Suburban population exploded, and the school district where I would be attending school grew so rapidly that they could not build classrooms fast enough. The district was forced to reopen several one and two-room schoolhouses, where they put the fifth graders. That year, at a one-room school just a mile from my new home, I enjoyed the best academic school year in my entire education. We had a fantastic teacher, and I was challenged to excel. The experience of an excellent teacher with only twenty students in the same room allowed me to grow academically.

In other critical ways, it was one of the worst years. Recess was a totally different story from the classroom. Because we had only one teacher, our playground break was largely unsupervised. The unguided playground experience of the fifth-grader can be cruel, children can be sadistic bullies, and relationships can be ugly. Boys' sense of their own masculinity tends to be determined primarily from participation in organized sports. Small, uncoordinated, and without athletic skills, I was consistently the last boy chosen for sports teams. The problem with being picked last by your peers is not that it happens once, but that it happens again and again. Feeling less competent when I compared myself to my peers in social areas – and for fifth-grade boys, sports are the key social area – I developed feelings of inferiority and low self-esteem.

Thus, I learned that I could be successful academically, but that sports and peer relationships were not areas where I excelled. I loved the classroom. I cringed when it was time for recess. At home I immersed myself in reading and solitary games. I knew the statistics of almost every major league player, but could not catch a ball.

CHAPTER 3

Life at Home

EMOTIONS MEASURE THE VALUE OF things and unconsciously guide us through life. I grew up in a home where emotions were not expressed. I don't recall being hugged by either parent. Kisses were a perfunctory peck on the cheek by my mother or grandmother. "I love you" was said with the same level of emotion as "How are you." It had no meaning. Other emotions were not expressed or encouraged either. Parents who are not in touch with their own emotions cannot model those feelings for their children. Emotionally, I was being prepared to enter the business world. Successful men and women in the corporate world generally have learned to quash their emotions and get the job done – to confront the facts and look for solutions. If you're unhappy with your boss or coworkers, you swallow that anger and do your job. I was also being prepared to be an addict. As I later learned, most people with addictive tendencies have learned to bury their emotions, rather than express them properly.

I struggle to explain my mother to the reader or even to myself. She was a bitter woman who could and did sarcastically rip apart anyone she felt was less important than she was. Service personnel, children, people of color and Jews, poor people or others less well-off, all were all victims of her viciousness. As a child, I was often so embarrassed by her outbursts that I wanted to hide and not be seen with her.

I remember my mother as obsessively authoritarian, emotionally withdrawn, and psychologically unavailable. Mother's reaction to a crying baby was to put the baby in his room and close the door. For Mother, nothing was ever quite perfect enough; an A- on my report card should have been an A, and an A should have been an A+. I worked to be good so I could avoid the criticism that made me feel like a failure, but I could never be good enough. Extremely autocratic, my mother was only happy when she was in control of herself and everything around her. She returned or exchanged every gift my father ever gave her. It was never right or good enough. She picked out the clothes my father was to wear each day. Mother was obsessively concerned about what other people might think. Dad was comfortable wearing anything. He never argued, just dutifully put on the clothes my mother had selected.

Mother never learned the old adage to "praise in public, criticize in private." Everything was done in public. I have a teenage memory of mother running out of the house to ask me, in front of my friends, if I had brushed my teeth. I was horrified. One friend described my mother as being "full of hot beans." I did not invite my friends to my house; I went to theirs.

Mother was more concerned with our home being a beautiful, well-kept place to show off to the neighbors than she was with it being a nurturing place for her three children. Our large, formal living room was mother's pride and joy. Children were not allowed in the living room. Footprints were not permitted. The nap in the carpet all lay in the same direction. I grew up believing that my mother cared more for her fancy living room than she did for me.

My father never got over the pain of the Depression, of dropping out of college to save a troubled business. The Depression colored the way he thought about life. Like many men in those days, business came first; running the family was left to the women. Even at home he kept a tight hold on family finances, not cheap, but not extravagant either. Mother never knew how much the family income was until Dad died years later. Emphasis on the business kept Dad busy. I recognized that work was his way of escaping the pressures of home. It was a lesson I learned early in life, and an example I followed for many years.

Am I being judgmental or unbalanced? Children are frequently critical and unjust toward their parents. I can only relate how I felt at the time. My mother did not intend to abuse me, but I was emotionally abused nonetheless. As noted by John Bradshaw in his book *Healing the Shame that Binds You,* when we don't learn from our parents how to relate in a family, how to be intimate, how to have emotional and intellectual boundaries, how to cope and solve problems, how to be self-disciplined, and how to love, we end up not being able to do those things. I never learned them.[iv]

Did my parents love each other? I'm sure they did in their own way. They were both excellent bridge players and played together frequently. They didn't fight or argue, at least not in front of their children. But their attachment was reserved, never openly emotional or affectionate. I saw no real intimacy and found little positive to learn from their relationship.

My brother, David, was only a few years younger than I was; my sister, Louise, was a year younger than David. Yet I felt as if I grew up as an only child. Louise and I were good students; David struggled in school. I would learn later that his intelligence lay in other areas. Each of us grew up in our own way. Louise and I shared anger and resentments, although she was the youthful rebel and I was the "good boy," holding it in – typical for a first born.

As a child I had all the material things I needed and most of the material things I wanted. But there was a lack of intimacy, and I grew up not knowing the warmth of loving or touching. Years later, David wrote of his childhood that he was "refreshed by some good memories of a good family and a simple way of life." Louise reports she has no memories of a single conversation with our father, and her only memories of our mother are of her screaming at her. We grew up in the same home. My memories of life at home include few memories of confidence or joy. I didn't feel loved as a child at home. Would there ever be enough love to make up for what I did not receive as a child?

CHAPTER 4

Success

IN THE SIXTH GRADE EVERYONE took the Iowa Test for Scholastic Achievement. Our teacher, Miss Foss, announced the names of the boy and girl with the highest scores. I was the boy. Student council elections were held the next day; one girl and one boy were to be chosen. I was elected. I was recognized for being intelligent, a talent I received from God or genes, but had little to do with achievements or social skills. Beyond school grades, IQ does not predict performance. People with high IQs do not have better relationships or marriages. There is little relationship between IQ and success in life. Robert Trivers notes in *The Folly of Fools* that intelligent people are more likely to deceive themselves. More than 90% of academics think they are in the top half of their profession. Smart people are seldom the most popular, and my short-term popularity did not last

I continued my active participation in our church youth group, and at the appropriate age I was confirmed as a member of the church. I did not have a sudden conversion experience; I had always been a Christian. I attended church camp and experienced the feelings of awe of worshiping in the outdoors. A few of my church friends formed a small band in which I played the piano. We weren't very good, but that didn't seem to matter. It was a place where I belonged.

My other social success revolved around my participation in the Boy Scouts. I loved camping, loved the outdoors. My first camping weekend as a full-fledged Boy Scout involved each of us cooking our own dinner. Dessert was an apple stuffed with marshmallow and chocolate. I removed the core of the apple with my Scout knife, along with a large amount of flesh between my left thumb and forefinger. I watched the muscle beat, then the blood pour out. A thirty-minute drive to the hospital and a few stitches later, I was given the choice between going home and returning to the campout. I did not hesitate. The baked apple was delicious.

Our Scout troop went camping each month and spent two weeks every summer at Scout camp. Challenges and difficulties came in boy-sized integers, able to be conquered, and brought with them a feeling of success. Every event brought its own obstacles – rain and floods, overturned canoes, cold and snow. These challenges allowed me to grow in strength and self-esteem. Scout patrols (I was in the Beaver Patrol) had to work together – buying food, setting up camp, cooking, fire building, and clean-up. We worked together in challenges and competition with other patrols and troops in First Aid, map and compass, and outdoor campcraft. I learned to follow, and to participate in activities that did not require being the biggest, strongest, and most coordinated. My weaknesses in athletics were not weakness in Scouts. I accepted responsibility and learned that the possibility of success was there for me. I was not a leader; that came later. I was a member, a fellow, a part of something bigger than myself. I was a Scout.

CHAPTER 5

Trauma

I MAY HAVE BEEN A successful Scout. But I was still a small, immature, unfinished boy not yet even showing signs of manhood. Freshman gym class took place during the first period of high school -- athletics and group showers. I remember hating dodge ball: other students throwing a ball at me as hard as they could, a ball I was afraid of catching. What fun was there in playing a game that was painful? The larger, stronger students thought it was fun. I was on the receiving end of the pain.

Not only was I not athletic, I was the only boy in the class without a hair on my body. I was viciously bullied because of my physical immaturity. I can still see myself standing in mind-grabbing terror in the corner of the shower, cowering and embarrassed. Bigger boys were snapping towels at me like whips, and savagely calling me names, as fourteen-year-old boys can do. My stomach tightened, and I wanted to throw up. I faced the yellow-tiled wall, hands covering my eyes, unsuccessfully hoping that the other boys could not see the tears streaming down my face. For the first of many times, I screamed inside, "I just want to be normal, like everyone else." I was ashamed – ashamed of my body, ashamed of crying, ashamed I was not good enough. I was too ashamed to tell anyone, beginning a life of secrets kept because of shame.

The harassment did not stop. Could being brutally taunted by peers attempting to assert their own dominance have contributed to later life difficulties? Years later, the sound I still heard was the laughter, taunting, and ridicule aimed at a little boy trying to hide in the corner of a group shower. I became a driven man, still trying to escape memories I did not want.

The bullying continued for several months. For the most part, the teacher was in his office, staying away from the showering boys. Occasionally he would come into the locker room and grab the genitals of some of the (fully dressed) more mature boys, telling them he was giving them their "Christmas goose." Immature boys were not worthy of even this dysfunctional attention.

When basketball season came, I decided to try out. If I was on the team, I would not have to go to gym class. Of course, there's not much need for short, skinny, uncoordinated boys on a high school basketball team, and as the time came for the games to begin I was cut from the team. I wasn't told to go back to gym class, so I went to study hall instead. It was well after basketball season when the gym teacher realized I wasn't attending class. By then things had calmed down.

It was only after I entered treatment years later that I recognized the bullying as sexual abuse. I was bullied because of my sexual immaturity, bullied for something I hated about myself, and bullied for something I would have changed in a heartbeat if I could. Our sense of our sexuality is deeply rooted, and sexual abuse can create deep shame. During high school, the peer group replaces the parent as the most important factor in a child's life. Not being physically endowed can be disastrous for a boy. It was for me.

Everyone is affected differently by abuse, and it may be difficult to understand how someone else feels. Researcher David Finkelhor[v] reported that "There have been many reports of adults with substantial psychological problems which seem very plausibly connected to a history of child sexual abuse." I was one of them.

Because sexuality is highly personal, sexual violations impact the victim's sense of himself or herself. The victims often fail to develop appropriate self-esteem and they allow their sense of worth to come from other people. They thrive on praise, engage in risky behaviors to get attention, and may act out sexually[vi]. I have spent much of my life trying to satisfy others, trying to be in the in-group of men and boys, like those in that gym class. Unfortunately, even while defining their self-worth worth externally, adults who were abused as children often have lost their ability to trust others and they greatly fear the intimacy that they also crave. They all too often find they can never get close to the people they so admire. The experiences of childhood shape our future patterns of reacting and relating to others. Some are good, some not so good.

Like many American boys, I wanted a hunting rifle like the ones my Grandfather J. owned. My parents were city raised, but chose to live in the country. Eventually they gave in, and I received an air powered 22-caliber rifle for Christmas. I was fifteen years old. On a cold, sunny January day, I took my new rifle and headed into the snow-covered fields near our home to find some rabbits. I could see tracks in the snow and followed them, hoping to scare up an animal. A rabbit jumped out from a clump of brush into the snow in front of me. I raised my rifle to my shoulder, aimed, and pulled the trigger. There was a blow to my head, and I stumbled backward. It felt as if somebody had hit me with a sixteen-pound sledgehammer. I knew I had been shot and looked across the field to see who had shot me. There was nobody else. Perhaps the gun had malfunctioned. Blood was everywhere, on my coat and pants, and on the ground in front of me. I was covered from head to toe. Surprisingly, I was conscious and aware. If I had been knocked out cold I could certainly have frozen to death in the zero-degree weather. Yet I could feel no pain. I walked a quarter mile to the nearest house, the Millers'. Thankfully, the Millers had eight children, and Mrs. Miller had seen blood before. She grabbed a bunch of towels, loaded me in her car, and drove me home. I felt excited, and neither depressed nor afraid.

I walked in the back door of the house. Mother was standing in the kitchen. I said, "Hi, Mom," but she was busy cooking and didn't look up. "I've been shot." Mother screamed and called for my dad. Dad drove me thirty-five miles to the nearest hospital at breakneck speed. The doctors put a stitch in my eyebrow and told me I had hit my head with the butt of the rifle. I knew better.

After an hour sitting in the emergency room, waiting for my family physician to arrive, I began vomiting. The emergency room doctors decided to x-ray my head. After the x-ray, I was told I had lost a lot of blood and should stay in the hospital overnight. Periodically a doctor would come into my room and run the back side of a reflex hammer down my foot. It felt like a hard rubber ball. Three days later the back of the hammer felt like a knife cutting the bottom of my foot. I had come out of shock. A doctor showed me the x-ray. The bullet had struck my left eyebrow, had passed through the frontal lobe of my brain, and was lodged in the left parietal lobe. It could not be removed.

I was lucky to be alive. The bullet passed within an eighth inch of the optic nerve, but I could still see. I could have been paralyzed, but I was not. I stayed in the hospital while the nurses fed me penicillin to prevent infection. After thirty days, I went home, apparently as good as new. I had survived a near-fatal accident and quickly resumed normal activities.

To this day, I am not sure what happened. The police investigated the gun and found no evidence that it malfunctioned. I have no memory or history of depression, nor any history of suicidal thoughts. The bullet is still intact, and still in my brain, over fifty years later.

CHAPTER 6

Wings

CHILDREN NEED WINGS AND ROOTS. They need the willingness and interest to get out in the world and explore, but the knowledge that they can always return to safety at home. Parents need to establish the secure emotional bonds that children can fall back on in times of stress. To me, home was not an emotionally secure place. My father fled to his job. Mother was an insecure perfectionist who could not be satisfied. I am critical of my parents for many things, but I'm grateful that they encouraged me to reach out, to leave home, and to travel. Scouting provided me my first major opportunity to go from home to places that provided the emotional safety I needed, and the opportunity for a small, immature boy to begin to grow. It also provided a way to escape an unhappy home.

As we entered high school, my scouting friends and I decided to organize an Explorer post, the Scouting program for teenage boys. In Exploring, less leadership came from the adult leaders and more from the boys themselves. The experience provided an opportunity that changed my life, and gave me a vision of my future. At least one weekend per month and every summer for the next four years were filled with new adventures.

Exploring allowed me to develop leadership skills. Surrounded by a group of supportive friends, I was elected president of our Explorer post. We planned and conducted activities throughout the Midwest. I was also chosen as the youth leader of the Explorer posts for our area. Our first event was a January campout at a new Scout camp not far from home. Over one hundred Explorers attended. The first night the temperatures dropped to near forty degrees below zero. In the morning, still in my sleeping bag, I had to reach down and pull on my feet to get my ankles to bend. There were only eight of us still in camp on the second night, ready for another night outside at forty below zero.

We usually combined our weekend trips with a stop on Sunday morning at a local church. We tried to visit different denominations. Most of the Explorers belonged to mainline Protestant or Roman Catholic churches. One weekend we hiked a lengthy wooded trail. On the way home we stopped at a small, conservative Baptist church out in the country. After a fire-and-brimstone sermon by the preacher, we were mobbed by the congregation's teenage girls who invited us to Sunday school and wanted to know if we'd been saved. Most of us weren't sure what that meant, but we agreed we certainly had been saved and left before the girls asked any more embarrassing questions.

To travel and participate in the adventures I loved, I needed money. An ad in *Boys' Life Magazine* led me to a solution. "Sell personalized Christmas cards. Excellent commission." I had been selling door-to-door since I was very young – fire extinguishers, spot remover, scissors. I loved sales. I worked for two card companies, three or four nights a week–for two months every fall, and averaged $50 profit per night. That was more than enough money to meet my needs for the year.

The summer after my freshman year of high school, the Explorers traveled to Ely, Minnesota, on the Canadian border, for a week of challenging canoeing in the Boundary Waters Wilderness. Paddling a canoe into three-foot waves and carrying an eighty-pound canoe on my back on a portage over muddy, slippery trails built self confidence that before I had found only in the classroom.

We camped on an island in the middle of a wilderness lake, fishing and watching a bald eagle soaring overhead, listening to the crazy call of a loon in the evening. We had not seen another soul in two days and decided to skinny dip in the cold, shallow, sandy-bottom bay near our campsite. No sooner were we in the water than three canoes of Girl Scouts glided around the bend. I expect they had a good laugh over twenty naked teenage boys scattering for cover.

Philmont is a 137,000-acre ranch in the Sangre de Cristo Mountains of New Mexico, where teenage Boy Scouts can challenge themselves during twelve-day mountain backpacking trips. I was fortunate to hike there three times during high school. On our second day on the mountain trails we climbed a very steep pass. I remember grabbing roots and tree limbs to pull myself up; I felt the satisfaction of knowing I could accomplish a challenging physical task. Later that trip, after carrying a fifty-pound pack on my back up an 11,000-foot mountain in a blinding rainstorm, we held a Sunday church service on the top of the mountain. Later we hiked down a narrow canyon in knee-deep mud during a flash flood, rolled out our sleeping bags to sleep, and woke up, cold and wet, having been carried ten feet downstream by the flowing mud. I rode on horseback past a coiled and angry rattlesnake, killed the snake with a rock, skinned it, and carried the drying skin on the back of my pack for a week. It proudly hung on the basement wall at home for years.

These demanding experiences led to growth and self-confidence, and I became known for my determination to take on and conquer tough challenges. Scouting gave me a way to grow my wings, away from the oppression of home, along with a chance to reach out, develop friendships, and try new things. That was a big change from being known as the skinny, immature freshman

The Explorers talked about purchasing a cabin in the Canadian wilderness as a permanent fishing destination. A teacher at our high school owned a resort on a remote lake in northern Ontario, where he took boys from the school for summer fishing adventures. He mentioned there was a decent cabin for sale on a nearby lake, a short portage from his lodge. My friend Stephen and I decided to go to his resort, portage over, and take a look. The teacher drove us to Red Lake, Ontario, where we boarded a bush plane and flew into the wilderness, landing on pontoons on a small bay near the lodge. It was my first time on an airplane. We tossed our gear in a cabin, climbed into a boat, and began fishing along the shore near the lodge. Within fifteen minutes, Stephen caught a ten-pound northern pike and I caught a six-pound walleye. Like the fish, we were hooked.

The next day Stephen and I portaged our boat to the nearby lake to look at the cabin. It was a beauty, a two-story log cabin right on the lake with a nice dock. It was unlocked, so we checked it out. We were impressed. It had solid floors, well-built airtight windows, and a roof that appeared to be weatherproof. Around the corner from the cabin was a small lodge and store, the only one in miles. We stocked up on candy bars and headed north across a large bay to fish.

After stopping to eat the lunch we had brought with us, we hiked along a small, sparkling stream into the Canadian wilderness. In time we came to an aspen grove. A gentle breeze was blowing through the leaves, and the sun shone through the trees with a bright, dazzling light. We both stopped and stared in amazement into the forest, in awe at the astonishing beauty. I knew I could see God shining white in the trees. For several minutes we stood and absorbed in wonder the sight in front of us. After a time, Stephen and I quietly returned to the boat. We said nothing to each other. What would I say? "Did you see God there in the woods?" Stephen would think I had lost my mind.

The next year the Explorers decided to spend a week at the cabin, although Stephen was not able to join us. I wrote the owner. He wanted to sell the cabin for $600 and was glad to let us use it for a week to decide if we wanted to buy it. I made the trip back up the stream and into the woods, but it was not the same. The patch of trees looked like any other forest. Reality set in for the Explorers, the cost of equipment and maintaining the cabin was beyond our means. We did not buy the cabin.

When I got home, the first thing Stephen asked was if I had gone back into the forest. Although we had not talked about it at the time, I knew then that Stephen had also seen God in the forest in northern Ontario.

Despite the challenges at home, my last two years of high school were fun and exciting. I performed in a high school play as a straight man in a very funny comedy, where I met Donna. She became my new girlfriend and I began smoking because she did – my first addiction. After school, the guys from Exploring cruised town in Gene's 1949 Hudson, with the windows wide open and Del Shannon's "Runaway" playing on the radio at full volume. The Hudson only got six miles to the gallon, but gas was seventeen cents per gallon, so we could drive all afternoon on the change left over from our high school lunch money.

And so, in high school, I began to develop wings. I learned to escape an unhappy home and find enjoyment and adventure in nature and the great outdoors. I developed the self-confidence that I lacked as a younger boy. I made friends and learned relationship and leadership skills. I became an Eagle Scout. I was no longer the same terrified boy who had entered high school.

CHAPTER 7

Where Am I Going?

UNFORTUNATELY, THINGS AT HOME WERE no better. Mother had not changed. I moved from a large, warm bedroom that I shared with my brother to our unheated screened porch, where I slept summer and winter. Even the cold northern winters could not impede my desire to escape from my family.

As time approached to decide where to go to college, my dad encouraged me to go to an outstanding university not far away. For me, it was too close to home. My neighbor, Mr. Evans, was a graduate of an Ivy League university in the Northeast United States. He encouraged me to apply there. I knew my test scores were good enough, although my grades were lower than it normally took to be selected. Mr. Evans knew that the university had a special admission program for students with good test scores and demonstrated leadership ability whose grades were a little low. I applied, and somewhat to my surprise, was accepted. The desire of a young adult to leave home is healthy, but I was not simply leaving home for college. I was fleeing, a pattern I developed in high school that would continue for much of my life. My choice of university was based more on the distance from home than it was on the academic excellence of the school. I was about to enter a totally new world.

In high school I had enjoyed my extracurricular activities more than studying. The university got what it should have expected, a student who did not let his book learning interfere with his education: I spent more time in my community activities than I did studying. Intelligence was no longer an advantage; I was one reasonably bright student among many as intelligent or more so. I was ill-prepared academically compared with students who had spent their lives laying the groundwork for an Ivy League education. I was used to being able to study on my own and doing well on the papers and exams. Now I had entered an environment of students who were accustomed to sharing ideas and helping each other learn. Those were skills I had not developed. I was in over my head. The first lesson I learned was humility.

I was housed in an ivy-covered dormitory. It was four stories tall with a lounge on the first floor, a stairwell up the middle, and four two-man rooms around the stairway on each floor. If the students in one room decided to party, the noise went up and down the stairwell. Soon we all joined in the festivity. My first leadership position was telling. Elected the dormitory chaplain – the keeper of the spirits – I was responsible for the dormitory bar, storing the liquor and hiring the bartenders for Friday and Saturday nights. Our housing unit historically had the lowest grade point average of any dormitory in the university. We continued the tradition.

Academically I struggled, changing majors again and again. Finally, I discovered that the English department had some great professors, and they would give me a degree for reading! I and finally settled on English as a major.

In an academic environment where I was a poor fit, I needed to find a place where I belonged. I found my place in politics. I became a leader in the campus libertarian organization, a conservative group. We brought speakers onto campus. A private dinner with William F. Buckley, Jr., was a highlight. Still early in the Viet Nam War, the American public believed that students should pay their tuition, study, and shut up. The university encouraged liberal activism and provided coffee and donuts to students protesting the war. I picketed the donut stand.

I joined the Young Republicans in our college town and soon became their president. Like many college towns, ours was very liberal and very Democratic, a real challenge for some idealistic Young Republicans. We succeeded in electing a city councilman and even a Republican governor. An attempt to elect one of our own as a State Representative was a learning experience. Even our candidate's relatives were afraid to ask for a Republican ballot in the primary election; too many had patronage jobs with the city or state and were afraid of losing their jobs if they registered as Republicans.

My interest in politics continued unabated. I traveled throughout the Northeastern United States in support of Barry Goldwater's effort to secure his Republican presidential nomination. In March 1964, during my spring vacation, I hitchhiked to Manchester, New Hampshire, to help Goldwater's campaign in the New Hampshire primary. I checked into a $5 hotel room, walked to campaign headquarters, and volunteered. I spent the day stuffing campaign brochures into envelopes. As I left that evening, I was handed a key and asked if I could open the office in the morning.

In the evenings I normally went wherever Senator Goldwater was speaking, escorted by a good-looking female reporter from the *New York Post* who drove a Jaguar XKE sports car. She was taking advantage of my knowledge of Goldwater's schedule and my ability to get front-row seats. I was riding around New Hampshire with a good-looking woman in a fancy sports car!

Henry Cabot Lodge, a write-in candidate from nearby Massachusetts, defeated Barry Goldwater and Nelson Rockefeller in the primary. Goldwater won the presidential nomination, but clearly was not going to win many electoral votes in the Northeast. I concentrated my efforts on successfully electing Republicans to the city council and other local offices. The local Republican Party recognized my efforts. I was elected to the Young Republican National Committee.

My parents were both excellent card players, and I had learned to play from them. Early in my college years I watched a poker game in which a student lost his car to another student. I didn't have a car. I vowed I would never gamble while I was at college. Several years later a young man asked me if I played gin rummy. I had played since I was a small boy. I agreed to play gin rummy with my acquaintance and promptly won several hundred dollars from him. The next week he asked me to play again. I reminded him how much he had lost the last time and that I expected he would lose again. He was not discouraged, and again I won several hundred dollars. This happened several more times, and I developed a reputation for being a good gin rummy player. Soon I was invited to play on weekends up and down the East Coast. I was gambling now. I continued to win; it was nice to have the extra cash I was accumulating. Every week my college acquaintance asked me to play. Every week I told him I was going to beat him, and week after week I won. This went on for about six months, until finally one night he won $200 from me. I never saw him again.

My grandfather died and left a small estate, and my parents decided to use the inheritance to take the entire family to Europe. They sailed to Europe on the *Queen Elizabeth II*. I had previously agreed to be in Miami at the Young Republican National Convention on the day my family was leaving for Europe. The conservatives were battling to take leadership of the Republican Party from the Eastern moderate establishment. We were successful in our bid to gain leadership of our party. I flew to London, arriving the day before my family, but missing the ocean voyage.

The fellow sitting next to me on the flight to London was a South African about my age. About 6'6" and weighing about 250 pounds, he had crewed on a sailboat across the Atlantic Ocean from Cape Town to the Caribbean. He was stopping in London and Paris on his way back to Cape Town. The airplane landed in the early afternoon, and we agreed to meet that evening and tour some of the parts of London I would never see with my parents. That was something I wouldn't have done without a companion his size. We went into illegal gambling clubs, saw groups of homosexual men congregating in the street, and watched a fight between rival gangs. These were new experiences for an unsophisticated young man who had grown up in the country. Years later, as a practicing sex addict, I would venture into similar neighborhoods, my fear overridden by my craving for illicit sex.

The European trip was interesting and broadening. One Friday night in Amsterdam I broke away from my family to visit Europe's largest red-light district. I was surprised to find young women displaying their bodies in large picture windows, as well as on the street. The Salvation Army Band marched up and down Canal Street, trying to save a few souls. I didn't participate, but I was once again exposed to a sordid lifestyle I had barely imagined.

I was particularly fascinated by the Berlin Wall, and the contrasts between East and West Berlin. The wall had been built in 1961 by the East Germans, who were trying to stop the "brain drain" of educated families leaving the communist state for the freedom and opportunity of the West. West Berlin was alive, vibrant, and dynamic; traffic jammed the streets. A guided trip into East Berlin showed me the difference. East Berlin was cold, silent, prefabricated; the wide, eight-lane streets were empty for blocks.

My last night in West Berlin, I walked along the wall, trying to comprehend it. I met an elderly German man who spoke no English. I speak no German. Passionately, he showed me where the wall had closed off the door of his church, now cold and empty. His wife was buried in a cemetery on the other side of the wall. He could not visit her grave. We spoke for almost an hour as he told the story of every bullet hole in the nearby buildings, and which East Berliners were killed trying to climb the wall, and which escaped to freedom. He showed me where some East Berliners had dug a tunnel under the wall, several hundred feet from the basement of one house to the basement of another. Twenty-two escaped before the tunnel was discovered. It was an enlightening conversation that taught me how unimportant language is to communication. In forty years I would meet another wall designed to keep people in – at a federal prison. That time I would be on the other side of the wall.

We continued our vacation through Austria, Switzerland, Italy, and France, finishing the trip in Paris. It was a thrilling and exhausting trip, but after ten weeks in Europe, I was ready to return for my last year of college, and to face decisions on the direction of my life.

CHAPTER 8

A Seemingly Unimportant Decision

THE VIET NAM WAR WAS important to many young men my age. We were expected to participate. If I was a full-time student, I was exempt from the draft that was selecting young men to fight. I knew our country was going to be at war long after I graduated. Since not all young men would be needed, our country's leadership determined to hold a lottery. Birthdates would be drawn. The young men whose birthdates were picked first would be the first drafted. My birthday was the seventeenth date drawn. I was going to war.

Unlike many of my peers, I was a staunch anti-communist and had no philosophical objection to the View Nam War. I did, however, want to fight as an officer. I attempted to enlist in the Marine Corps Officer Candidate School program. What was I thinking? I weighed 105 pounds and had no athletic ability whatsoever. I flunked the physical. More reasonably perhaps, I attempted to enlist in the Air Force Officer Candidate School, but the results were the same. I expected I would be drafted after I graduated, although I hoped I would not. Perhaps the bullet in my head would keep me out. The uncertainty weighed on me.

One day, on the way back from one of my political jaunts, I drove past an adult movie theater. I was twenty-one years old and had never been in an adult theater. My only exposure to pornography was *Playboy*. Tempted, I drove around the block, looking at the pictures of almost naked men and women in posters outside the theater. I was a naïve young man, a virgin with no sexual experience: a Christian. Sex should be saved for marriage, I thought.

But I was twenty-one; going into an adult theater was legal now. Curiosity won out. I parked and went into the dark theater.

The film had been running for some time, but I quickly learned that didn't matter. The film had no plot. On the screen men and women were engaging in sexual activity beyond anything I had ever imagined. I watched until I had seen the entire film.

After watching the movie, I made a decision that seemed completely unimportant at the time. I went to the men's room in the basement to urinate before driving home. In the restroom were three young men who appeared to be doing nothing. As I stepped to the urinal, a tall, slender young man came to the urinal next to mine and began masturbating. Why had he picked the urinal so close to mine? I did not intend to watch him, but I did. I could not help myself, and I became aroused. He said nothing, but he knew I was watching and he signaled me to join him in a toilet stall. I could not even imagine doing such a thing. But just like my experience as a four-year-old following the man into the woods, I did as he asked. His two friends guarded the door.

That was my first experience engaging in sexual activity with a stranger. I remember it clearly, like the alcoholic remembers his first drink. I had broken a moral code that I cherished, crossed a boundary I had promised never to cross. Yet I was so excited that I barely slept for several days. It would be years before my next experience with anonymous sex, but it would not be my last.

The fuse that ignited my sexual addiction was a cable woven of many threads. One thread was the violation of a young boy's boundaries by a stranger asking to see the boy's four-year-old penis. Another was an unhappy childhood -- with a workaholic father and a self-centered, perfectionist mother in a home where emotions were not expressed-- where healthy relationships and intimacy had no chance of being experienced because they were not present. Multiple threads were added as an intelligent child with limited athletic ability was picked last day after day on the playground, teaching the child that his self-worth came not from intrinsic, God-given value, but from what others thought of him. More threads were braided in with childhood lessons *about* God without learning to *know* God, and with the shame, confusion, and pain of sexual abuse in the high school shower after gym class. Learning to run from problems, to escape rather than face them, strengthened the cable even more. But the match that lit the fire of that long fuse was struck in a basement toilet stall in a pornographic theater when I was twenty-one years old.

CHAPTER 9

Time to Move On

AFTER FOUR YEARS OF COLLEGE, it was time to leave a place where I could easily choose my direction, change it, and choose another. Graduation forced the big decisions on how I would spend the rest of my life. On one side was politics. An effort to obtain the Republican nomination for a competitive State Senate seat was thwarted by redistricting. I was offered the nomination for a safe Republican seat on the city council. At age twenty-two, serving in the city council would provide a launching spot for a political career, although not a very potent one.

I would also need a real job. City councilmen received a small stipend, but not nearly enough money to live on. I approached a friend, a man I respected for his work in politics, who owned a manufacturing company in the city. After I completed two batteries of tests, I was offered a job as an industrial salesman for $12,000 per year plus commissions. This was an excellent salary in those days for a young man straight out of college, but the job would require quite a bit of travel which would likely conflict with my political aspirations. Thankfully, he would not take my answer for two weeks.

I received an unexpected call from a man who remembered me from my time in high school. He was the head of a nonprofit organization that was attempting to influence and improve public education. He had heard I was looking for a job and offered me a position over the telephone. He described the job, and the more he talked the more excited I became. I believed that public education was failing many of the families it should have been helping. I would be showing people a new way of life. The job would require some traveling and a lot of independence. I saw excellent opportunities for growth. I gave up politics and turned down a $12,000-a-year job selling valves for a $6,000-a-year job selling ideas. It was an unexpectedly easy decision.

Six weeks later I was back in the Midwest, living in a smaller community that was a three-hour drive from the rest of my family. A town of about 12,000 filled with people who cared about one another was an ideal place for me to begin my career. I rented a small house on the edge of town. A nerve-racking bus trip to the draft physical, carrying the x-rays showing the bullet still in my brain, resolved the issue of going to Viet Nam. I flunked the physical and felt free to begin my adult life.

My new job and I were a fit from the first day. The day before I went on the payroll I was given a syllabus and asked to help lead a seminar for some school board members. I loved it. I was a young man only a few weeks out of college, but I discovered I had a talent for speaking. People who were much older than I responded to my message – a message I believed in. I knew I would make a difference in the lives of others. A person who has a job they enjoy and that they believe is making the world a better place is very fortunate. I was.

One of my neighbors was a local surgeon, Dr. Nicholas Eldridge, an enthusiastic outdoorsman. We became good friends. We hunted and fished together, and I often found myself at his home at meal time. Dr. Nick and his wife Mary, also a physician, had four children. I felt as though I had found a new home.

I occasionally dated a girl from a local college, but she graduated and moved away. My friends were almost all older than me. Drs. Nick and Mary knew a young lady they thought I should meet, and they invited Ellyn and me to dinner at their home. Ellyn also worked at the local hospital.

People make snap judgments about a person's likeability, honesty, and competence within seconds of meeting them, and rarely revise their first impression. My first impression of Ellyn was that she was friendly and attractive, but I could tell she didn't feel well, and I was a little shaky myself. Our first date was an evening to be remembered.

The night before our scheduled date, I was shopping at the local discount store when I ran into the Eldridges. They took one look at me and said, "You don't look too well." I didn't feel well either. He said, "Stop by my office tonight when you are finished shopping, and I'll fix you up." I left his office at 9:15 p.m. Friday with a bottle of some foul-tasting medicine to settle my stomach from the Hong Kong flu. The next morning Ellyn called the Eldridge's home to say she was too sick to go on a date. Determined, Dr. Nick told her he would pick her up and examine her at his office on the way to dinner. So, we met with Ellyn's bottle of medicine in my left sport coat pocket, my own in my right. We struggled through a quiet night of friendly conversation and were home in our own beds by 9:30.

Despite our shaky first date, Ellyn and I continued to see each other. Ellyn had a nice personality, and we had enjoyed each other despite feeling ill. She tells me she thought I'd dropped out of the sky. I was a college graduate who supported himself, living in her little hometown where most of her classmates either married right after high school or moved away. But after that short date when both of us were ill, she didn't think she'd hear from me again. I was not ready to give up without trying one more time. On our next date, we went to the movies. By our third date, dinner on New Year's Eve, we both knew our relationship had promise.

Ellyn's mother had died in childbirth when she was born. Pearl Harbor had been attacked, and Ellyn's father enlisted in the navy. He was sent to Hawaii to join the fight against Japan. She was raised by her elderly grandparents, who still had their daughter Elizabeth living at home. When Ellyn's father returned from the war he remarried, had two more children, and lived only a few blocks from Ellyn, who stayed with her grandparents. His bitterness and perfectionism caused him to be critical of those around him, particularly Ellyn. Like me, she felt that she could never be good enough. Elizabeth, eleven years older than Ellyn, had become pregnant and married when she was eighteen; therefore, Ellyn's grandparents had become extremely overprotective. She went to school and came home, never participating in after-school activities. She attended a local church, walking alone the few blocks from her home. Her grandfather, an electrician who had been employed by several local industries, died when Ellyn was eleven, leaving his family with little income. Other than two years when she attended community college twenty-five miles from home, Ellyn had lived with her grandmother in the same house her entire life.

Ellyn survived a bitter and rejecting father. She was raised in an extremely sheltered and untrusting environment, essentially abandoned by both parents. Her childhood did not leave her with the confidence and hope to lead a happy and independent life.

Yet our relationship survived. We enjoyed each other's company and shared each other's conservative values. It was not long before we fell in love. I drove past her house when I didn't need to, wishing I was inside with her. We played card games, went to the movies and out to dinner. I put my head on her shoulder, and a jolt went through my body. I began to see Ellyn as someone with whom I could share my life. Apparently, she saw things the same way. We became engaged less than two months after our first date.

The year was 1968, a tumultuous one for American society and for our Midwestern community as well. As a conservative, I believed in personal action rather than government regulation, preferring to do things because they seemed right to me. I took liberal actions in a conservative way. I had become active in the civil rights movement and became friends with several of the local leaders in the African-American community. I became involved, attempting to help bring our divided community together. Martin Luther King was murdered on Good Friday, and racial tensions were high. Angry black teenagers roamed the streets of downtown; others stayed home with their parents, trying to avoid the trouble they knew was coming. Slowly things calmed down; trouble was delayed but not resolved.

Later that spring my company began integrating previously segregated programs and facilities. In June, we held a banquet at the previously all-white Elks Club for over three hundred teens and adults, half black and half white, to celebrate our accomplishments working together. The dinner was a huge success. After dinner several of the adults who had provided leadership to the program met at Dr. Nick's home for refreshments. Policemen, firemen, and local merchants representative of the community were present.

Our integrated group knew racial tensions were still high in town, and a police radio sat on the kitchen counter. Around 10 p.m. we heard that a group of young black men had firebombed a small convenience store and were heading toward the north end of town. Our group quickly scattered, back to work, to home, or to protect their property.

Ellyn and I remained at the Eldredge's because the rioters were heading straight down the street past her grandmother's house. The police broke up the riot after four or five buildings were firebombed, arresting a dozen young men, including relatives of those attending our dinner. We passed through three roadblocks before getting Ellyn home by 4 a.m. We couldn't miss the frustrating contrast: on the same night we celebrated our progress in integration, a dozen discontented young men expressed their own frustration through violent behavior and ended up in prison. Racial violence in our community ended in one night, but many of America's major cities were in flames.

After a six-month engagement, Ellyn and I were married in the local Methodist church. Our honeymoon, a three-week flying and driving trip through the western United States, was Ellyn's first time traveling more than a few hours' drive from home. We moved into my small home outside of town. Ellyn and I built a marriage on shared values, but brought into the marriage all the dysfunctions of our childhood. Ten months later I received an opportunity to work three hundred miles away in a very different community. As we drove north, miles from her hometown, Ellyn cried. For her, it was the first move of many, and the first time living away from her family. For me it was one more step in my career. Nine moves later, Ellyn said she would title her autobiography "Tales of a Transplanted Rose."

Most of my work now was in values education, showing parents and educators how to teach values to their children. I was developing a reputation as a young man who was expert in his field. I loved the work and spent more time at it than I should have. Speaking engagements kept me traveling most days and many evenings, away from my family.

Our oldest son, Brady Jr., was born, and we brought him home to our rented abode. We joined a church and served in leadership positions. Although we made friends and became part of the community, Ellyn felt very isolated, trapped at home with a young child while her husband was having a good time at work.

Our next move was to a larger city, where Ellyn and I were able to purchase our first home. It had three bedrooms, one bath, and a full unfinished basement. It was a brand-new home, so I had to put in the lawn. Ellyn made the draperies and we hung them together. I built a family room in the basement. The neighbors were friendly, and we fit right in. We were welcomed into our new church, where almost immediately I was asked to become church treasurer. Of course, I said yes. Moving was easy for me; I had a job and instant contact with new people.

At this point I have given you a description of my youth, and a little insight into my marriage and the beginning of my career. Although I had still not reached the age of thirty, the pattern of my life was established. Those experiences that, in time, led to my addiction had for the most part been embedded in my memory. Did I learn the path of compulsiveness from the self-centeredness and obsession of my mother; the lack of boundaries from the sexual abuse by a stranger? Did I fail to learn the traits of intimacy in a home where there was none, or fail to deal with emotion in a home where it was not expressed? Did I grow up convinced of my own worthlessness and ashamed of my body because of what I learned on the fifth-grade playground or in the ninth-grade locker room? Was there a neurological or traumatic component at work from the bullet to my brain? Did bullying teach me that I could not count on others, and intellect teach me too strongly that I could handle things on my own? Had I learned to avoid my family and escape to work like my father had, rather than face the challenges of difficult relationships? Had I learned of a distant God rather than one who knew me and related to me? Was the damage already done before I knew I was damaged? In retrospect, I can see that all of these cumulative factors had a role to play.

On the other hand, I had a good education, decent values, and good leadership skills. My childhood experiences of being last on the athletic field gave me a hunger that others may find difficult to comprehend, the hunger that drives one to seek success. I had a job I loved and a good work ethic. I had developed the wings I needed to reach out without fear and to welcome the unknown. I had a wife I loved, whose values I shared. You would think that would be good enough – strong enough – to overcome the negative experiences that I could not forget.

CHAPTER 10

Another Seemingly Unimportant Decision

I LOVED MY JOB AND enjoyed reaching out into the community, but times were tough and nonprofit organizations were struggling financially, including ours. One rather depressing afternoon, my boss and I left the office early and went to a nearby hotel bar. I told him that I thought the staff was too poorly organized to accomplish our mission, which led us into the financial difficulties we were facing. On a cocktail napkin, I sketched out a different organizational plan. He agreed. Much to my surprise, the executive board of our nonprofit corporation approved my plan. Even more shocking, I was promoted into a new management position, responsible for about half of our staff. That was to become a great learning experience.

Two years later we were still in business, but the dismal financial picture had not improved. The Executive Board hired a new CEO to fix the problem. His first major strategy was to eliminate two of the five mid-management positions, and all five of us were told to seek new jobs elsewhere. I wrote a new resume and began looking. A few months later the boss called me into his office. Two of our mid-managers had resigned, and responsibilities were reshuffled. I had a new job. I was the new chief finance and operations officer, responsible for all financial management and most staff supervision. With just over two years' management experience, I was not remotely qualified for this new assignment. I supervised staff scattered over a large geographical area. The remaining management staff was hard-working and dedicated. We liked and trusted each other. Were we good enough to save the organization? We didn't know.

We developed a plan to raise enough cash to pay off the organization's debt. It failed. We developed a second plan. It also failed. Refusing to give up, we developed a third plan. On the day before the third campaign was to begin, the boss summoned me once again. He had resigned, bought an accounting firm in Atlanta, and was leaving town the next day. He would be back in three weeks to clean out his desk. I was temporarily in charge. The new financial plan was brutal. The staff worked six days a week, fourteen hours a day. We sold assets and collected accounts receivable that were years old. The work was hard on the staff and their families, too, but when the boss came back three weeks later the organization's debt was gone. Our former boss was amazed. "If I had believed the plan was going to work," he said, "I wouldn't have resigned."

Two months later I had a new boss. The debt was gone and the job I had done forgotten. Programs were in disarray, neglected while we dealt with the financial issues, and my mentor was in Atlanta. In two months I had gone from being a hero to being a man who never should have been put in my position in the first place, who was considered marginal and in over his head. My job was in jeopardy.

I met with other management staff and developed a twelve-month plan to improve operations and program quality. I knew that if I slipped once along the way I would be looking for a new job. But the staff was strong, the plan was good, and the work was fun. The plan worked. In nine months our programs were strong and our reputation growing. School districts began approaching us to expand our programs.

Perhaps the work was too fun. When work becomes a compulsion, an irresistible impulse to perform an irrational act, it becomes workaholism. I began to spend time at work that I should have spent at home, time my wife and son needed from me. Then our second son, Fred, was born, and Ellyn felt even more trapped, stuck at home, while I was having fun working, she thought. She seemed not to understand the difficulty and importance of my job, or the stress I was under. Of course she didn't. I never discussed it with her. I didn't understand the depression she felt, isolated at home with two small children. My lack of empathy was one more sign of my addictive illness.

I knew I needed to spend more time with my family. Ellyn and I planned a three-week family camping vacation. We drove a van, where Ellyn and I slept, and bought a tent for the boys. The first night we stopped at my parents' house to celebrate my father's seventy-second birthday and our tenth wedding anniversary, which would be the next day. As we returned to my parents' home after dinner at 10:30 that evening, the telephone was ringing. The call was from a recruiter. He offered me a job interview, the opportunity to be the president of a small but troubled nonprofit in yet another city. Of course, the interview was in the middle of our long-awaited vacation.

On our tenth anniversary, we were rerouting our vacation so that by the interview date we were visiting old friends where Ellyn and the boys could stay. I told friends back home how to break into my house, find the clothes I needed, and ship them to me. Excited, I flew to a new city. The interview was hilarious. The volunteer Chairman of the Board of Directors, an attorney, had been fighting with the rest of the board. The committee of volunteers appointed to employ a new president had refused to tell the chairman the location of the meeting, and he did not attend. I was offered the job and accepted, then flew back to finish the vacation with my family.

This move was a difficult financial step. The new nonprofit organization was in a higher-cost-of-living area that more than consumed the salary increase I received. I could not afford to live near my new office. My parents' home was near the same city. Many families would be thrilled to live near their parents. We were not. Ellyn and I had already decided that we wanted to live far enough away that my mother would not drop in without calling first. We purchased a "handyman special" that was a thirty-minute drive from both my parents and my office. The anger from my childhood had not dissipated.

I don't believe any job is more difficult than running an almost-bankrupt small business. I had accepted a job to turn around an organization that had lost money for eight years in a row. My first day on the job I opened my desk drawer and found it full of checks, checks my predecessor had written to our suppliers but had not mailed. There was no money to cover the checks or to pay the outstanding bills. When my predecessor received a bill, he would write a check to pay it and put the check in his desk drawer. When money arrived, he decided which check to mail. Some of the checks in the drawer were two years old.

Although this organization was over fifty years old, everything was in disarray. There had been no effective planning. During the day I worked with our very small staff, trying to expand our programs and increase revenue enough to pay the bills. On evenings and weekends, I met with clients and studied the operation, trying to find ways to reduce expenses. The pressure I felt was immense; the whole weight of salvaging a sick company seemed to be on my shoulders. Slowly programs began increasing. We paid off some of our bills and added a few staff. There was still little time for my family. Stress, anxiety, and pressure dominated my life.

On the way to and from work, I passed a small, rundown XXX video store where pornographic movies and books were sold. For two years I had driven past that store without much thought. One day I stopped. The pressures of my job created a lot of anxiety for me, and I thought that perhaps looking at some pornography would help me relax and reduce that anxiety. I knew I should not go in, but I did anyway. It was another seemingly unimportant decision that I would later come to regret. I quickly discovered that not only were there booths to view pornography privately, but that people were engaging in sexual activity in the booths. Doors were left open so others could watch. My desire to participate was overwhelming. Having dismissed Ellyn's need to be more intimate, I needed to feel needed on a personal level, and I immediately recalled the ecstasy of my experience with a stranger in the men's room toilet stall sixteen years before.

I gave no thought to the effects my behavior might have on anyone else. Instead, I remembered the excitement of taking a risk and not being caught. I remembered the euphoria of feeling wanted, of being considered attractive. My memories went back to the first year of high school, when I was bullied and abused because of my sexual immaturity. Here, in these dingy booths in the back rooms of a porn store, I was desired. I was instantly hooked.

Everything about the store added to the thrill of being there. I enjoyed watching and being watched. Even the smell of stale smoke and perspiration-filled bodies was intoxicating. Occasionally the police would come to check for illegal activity. The clerk out front would blink the lights in the back, alerting us to get dressed, close the doors to the booths, and put more coins in the video machines. For a moment we were just customers spending a few dollars to look at pornographic videos. Then the police would leave. The danger from the possibility of being caught added to the intoxication.

Each day, entranced by the pornography and the anonymous sex, I would sheepishly tell myself, "I'm not going to stop at the video store today." However, I did. Thinking only of myself, ignoring that my wife and children needed me at home, I spent thirty minutes or an hour every day looking at pornography and engaging in sexual activity with people I did not know or care about, sex with no expectation of a continued or intimate relationship. I convinced myself that my actions reduced the stress of work. Yet I knew what I was doing was wrong. I hated myself for what I was doing. I was ashamed. I wanted to quit, but I could not. I was caught in a cycle of thoughts, feelings, and actions that I did not understand and could not control. I was a sick man.

I had been a person who prided himself on being able to control his life. Every day I faced challenges at work and found ways to overcome them. I loved telling others how to teach values to children. I was succeeding financially. Intelligent and educated, I was in a stable marriage with two terrific children. But I was living two lives, and the values I expressed in one life violated the values I held in the other life. I had become a sex addict, and I did not realize it.

After more than a year of stopping at the porn store, the shame I felt overwhelmed me. The emotional pain of my out-of-control behavior left me afraid and bewildered. I did not want to admit to anyone that I was engaging in deviant sexual behavior, but the pain was so great that I had to do something. I told my two best friends what I had been doing. I trusted them and felt confident of their friendship. At that point in my life, confiding in them was the most difficult thing I had ever done. Fortunately, they kept my confidence. However, life would get more difficult quickly. They both told me that I needed to tell my wife.

Ellyn was devastated. I had broken her trust and the vows I made when we got married. The husband she had hoped would be perfect was exposed as a man with serious flaws. I was afraid she would ask me to leave, but she did not. She cried for a long time, and for days she seemed to be in a trance. So was I. I attempted to rebuild my marriage, but the truth was I had no idea how to have a real intimate relationship with another person, even my wife. Neither of us had been raised in a home where intimacy was modeled.

We both tried therapy, but it did not seem to help much. In those days sexual addiction was not understood. I had stopped looking at pornography, and I no longer had sex with anyone other than my wife, but I still had my self-centered, addictive personality. Recovering alcoholics would have called it a dry drunk. I was worried about my job and myself more than I was worried about my wife and family.

After a few months life seemed to return to "normal." I went back to working too much, and Ellyn went back to college to receive the degree she had not completed years before. She hoped she could begin a career in a field she loved. We quickly stopped talking about my indiscretions, as if that would make them go away.

Unexpectedly, Ellyn became pregnant with our third child. Once again, her dreams were shattered. She was angry and afraid, yet she knew that for her, the only decision was to have the baby. Our two children were growing up, ages seven and eleven. Ellyn longed for more independence, for time to pursue her own path. Now we were moving forward on an unplanned road, and Ellyn's plans for a career were blocked. We also faced the challenges of a high-risk pregnancy, the increased possibility of a child with severe birth defects that comes with being older parents. Ellyn was afraid I would fall back into my old behavior, leaving her a single parent with three children.

Normally the best parts of our life together were our family vacations. When we were on vacation the problems of our home life seemed to disappear. That year we drove with the children to the far side of Lake Superior and then took the Polar Bear Express train north to Hudson Bay, so I could swim in the 36-degree water. The air temperature was 42 degrees, and even the local natives told me I was crazy. I dove into the bay; the frigid temperatures for just a moment diverted my thinking away from the uncertain future. As soon as our return train got back to a town that had a pay phone, we would make the call that would tell us if our baby would be healthy.

We both felt the anxiety of the upcoming phone call, the helplessness of knowing that whatever we would hear was out of our control. We found a pay phone in a small town on the edge of the Northern Ontario wilderness. The doctor told us we could expect a healthy baby boy. Larry was born five days after I interviewed to become the president of another larger, but broke, organization.

It was another strange interview. The new organization had serious financial problems and a history of poor leadership, starting with the Executive Board. I was not their first choice for the job. Several candidates had already turned them down. The board wanted an older, successful leader with experience leading a similar size nonprofit. They failed to realize that a person with that background would not want to do the same thing again.

After several months of trying to attract good candidates, they decided to focus on three men, including me, a thirty-nine-year- old hotshot who didn't fit their original profile. Again, they could not make a decision. I went home to participate in the birth of my third son Larry, not knowing if our family would be moving again. One week later I was told they had hired someone else. One of the board members later told me, "I voted against you because you've never had a big blow-up in your career. I was afraid you would have it here." His prediction was twenty years early.

Opportunities can take a funny path. Two weeks later I received another call from the headhunter. "Are you still interested?" Somehow the position was open. I still saw the job as a good opportunity. The company's weaknesses and my strengths matched well. "They're considering other candidates, but you have a lot of support. They'll contact you in a couple of weeks." I took the next day off to go with Ellyn and Larry to the doctor's office for his PKU test. When I came back to work the following morning there were a stack of messages on my desk. Once again, we were moving to a new community and a new job.

The new job was a step up. Although I had found that the larger the organization, the slower it is to change, I had been hired to right a sinking ship and for the most part was given the leeway to do that. The financial problems were not as deep as I had faced before, and the quality of the employees better than I had been told. One major staff change was all it took, and things started moving in the right direction. The organization expanded its program offerings, concentrating on values education programs that teachers could use in the classroom. I continued to conduct seminars and wrote inexpensive literature for children. I became more convinced that children were not learning good character traits at home. They had to be taught, and elementary and secondary schools were the place children could be found. My professional reputation continued to grow.

When the telephone rings at four am, it's never a good sign. It was my mother. My father had had an embolism in his sleep and died unexpectedly. I knew I could be the first of her children to arrive, and I was on an airplane to Florida in two hours. As we waited for the rest of the family to arrive, mother wanted to see Dad's financial records. She had never seen them and had no idea how the family money was invested. The records were in perfect order. Pasted between the pages of his ledger we found several thousand dollars in cash. Dad's fear of having no money, begun in the Depression, had followed him to his death. I was asked to give the eulogy at the small family service, but could not do it. Sadly, I did not know him well enough. I was unable to cry for my loss or my mother's.

I continued to spend extraordinary amounts of time at work. Ellyn continued to feel trapped at home with the children, and her depression grew. I was a problem solver and wanted to fix her problems, but nothing I did would make them go away. I felt responsible for her problems, and I'm sure I aggravated them. She needed someone to comfort her, a level of intimacy that was beyond my understanding or ability at that time.

Our children grew quickly. I enjoyed doing things with the boys, particularly outdoor activities. We hiked and camped together. Brady Jr. had a lovely singing voice, and Ellyn was very excited when he was chosen to participate in a highly selective High School Show Choir. Despite the many hours I worked, I seldom missed one of our children's activities. Those who looked at our family from the outside did not see the difficulties on the inside.

Toward the end of our son Brady's junior year of high school, I was invited to leave private nonprofit work and go to work for the state Department of Education in a Western state. This was a different opportunity. I was returning to politics but was expected to be nonpolitical. Brady needed one more year to finish high school, and Ellyn was living the positive experience she never had in high school through him. One more time, my career won out. I moved; Ellyn stayed behind to sell the house and move the family several months later.

My previous experiences were in heading small nonprofit organizations that were in financial trouble, where the executive board that hired me wanted decisive leadership from their new CEO. Changing a large, bureaucratic governmental organization was much more difficult than rescuing a smaller, failing nonprofit. But the state had hired me for a reason. I knew the direction they wanted to move, and they knew I wanted to move that way too. I enjoyed the challenge and, slowly, the changes were made.

The reader may notice that my self-image became based on my accomplishments at work. Yet my family seemed to do well. Ellyn's depression appeared to be less overwhelming. Our children adapted quickly to our new community, making new friends and succeeding in school, sports, and Scouts. Ellyn and I became leaders in our church, as we had in every community in which we lived. I was asked to be an elder, a lay minister for our local church. My assignment was to serve senior citizens in nursing homes. Ellyn and I served together. I was surprised to find the work very rewarding and felt comfortable that I was doing what God wanted of me. I continued my workaholic ways, and my reputation continued to grow.

The following year was my mother's eightieth birthday. She invited her children and grandchildren to Florida. At her birthday dinner, Mother got a little tipsy. When we returned to her home she invited the grandchildren to walk on her living room carpet where, as usual, the nap of the carpet was all carefully vacuumed in the same direction. It was a moment none of us has ever forgotten, the only time my children were allowed in my mother's living room.

After eight years in one job, I was ready for a change. I was proud of my accomplishments and was beginning to develop a national reputation. There were rumors that a large national nonprofit was considering inviting me to join their top management team. This would be a totally different experience for me, and I expressed interest in being considered. I attended a large trade show in Honolulu, where the top management of the organization in which I was interested was also participating. I thought perhaps I would be sounded out while I was there, but the conference ended without any contact. Ellyn and I planned to leave the next morning for a vacation in the Islands.

At 7 a.m. the telephone rang. It was the company CEO, inviting me to coffee in his suite. He was looking for someone to head marketing and communications, fields that I enjoyed. The job would involve a significant amount of travel. I would be spending half my time flying around the country. One more time we would be moving. We hoped it would be our last move.

CHAPTER 11

The Last Big Move – Sort Of

THIS WAS AN EASY MOVE. Our house sold the first day it was on the market. That wasn't unusual; Ellyn had become expert at preparing a house for sale. We quickly found a home in our new community and moved the day before Larry started school. He attended a brand-new school, and within two weeks he was elected to the student council. I quickly threw myself into the new job, leaving Ellyn to find her own way.

It didn't take long for me to recognize that this job was not what I had expected. For eighteen years I had worked for a supportive board of directors or a legislature. I was again in a nonprofit corporation, working for someone else. I had a huge responsibility, and a huge budget. But decisions were tightly controlled "upstairs." The company had a perfectionist culture, mistakes were not tolerated, and there was huge resistance to even the smallest change. My background was as a leader who could take risks and encourage strategic and creative change. They wanted someone who would protect their image and not mess things up. I don't blame them; I had accepted the wrong job.

I respected that this was a very traditional and highly structured organization. However, I saw an opportunity to change the way children were educated. My style required making waves; their style was to cooperate and get along. Even my smallest efforts to bring about strategic change were stymied. While I had developed good skills at leading and inspiring those who worked for me, my skills at upward communication in the organization were not strong enough. When I could cause change, it was change at the margins, not the strategic change I thought was needed. I became frustrated.

Ellyn began to find herself more isolated and often felt left out. I traveled more and worked more hours. Even though Ellyn had suffered from depression all her life, I blamed myself for her moods. She blamed me too. Ellyn was not good at asking for the things she needed, and I was not good at figuring them out. When she didn't get them, she became resentful. Just as she thought I should be able to make her happy, she thought she should be able to make me happy. When that didn't appear to work, she became even more depressed. When I could do nothing to make Ellyn happy, I grew frustrated, worked harder, and traveled more. Many nights I did not call home. I did not want to hear her depressed-sounding voice.

I became in demand as a speaker and traveled throughout the country speaking to educators, parents, and even politicians. I was an unhappy employee, but found that one of my primary duties was to make other people feel good about themselves and the things they were doing. I was surprisingly good at it. I was becoming talented at hiding my feelings and living an external life that was different from my internal life.

My mother passed away in Florida, several days before her ninety-second birthday. Unlike at my father's funeral, I was able to speak at mother's, but I did not cry. I realized I had not cried since I was abused in the high school shower forty years before. I still carried bitterness from my childhood, directed at both peers and parents. Mother had been a painter, and her paintings were well done. Shortly after her death, Ellyn hung one of mother's paintings in our bedroom. I felt unexpectedly angry. I had never dealt with the trauma of my childhood.

CHAPTER 12

Pornography

HOW IS IT THAT HUNDREDS of thousands of otherwise normal and decent men and women become attracted to and trapped in activities in which they never dreamed they would engage? Due to the freedom provided by the Internet, people are able to engage in behaviors they never would have considered. By making an apparently unimportant decision at the computer to relieve stress or boredom, they can enter a fantasy world that had been barely in their dreams: the world of pornography. They wish they hadn't. They hesitate, not sure why, repelled and yet curious, drawn by something they do not understand, and they are hooked. They do not have to go looking for it; it comes to them. If only they knew the effects certain events would have on their lives.

As I headed toward addiction, I had no idea what path I was taking. The more freedom I had, the less free I became. I soon found myself traveling about 150 days per year. In some ways the travel was enjoyable, but in other ways, I knew I was traveling to avoid the frustration I felt in the office and at home. My life felt stressful. We cannot easily change our emotions. However, holding emotions inside creates a poison that eats at your innermost being. Following years of experience, my ego was so strongly dependent on success in my career that when I no longer felt successful, and even though my boss was happy with my performance, I began unconsciously looking for other arenas.

My descent into addiction was not a rapid change; it came slowly over time. I had a lot of down time, lonely time. Pornography found me on a business trip, spending a boring evening alone in a hotel room. Playing on my computer, I wandered into a chat room populated by men talking about sexual issues. Someone sent me an instant message. "Do you have any pictures?" I knew they were looking for pornography. I answered, "No." It was several months and many business trips later when I answered the same question, "No, send me some." He did. I had ventured back into the world of pornography that I had left seventeen years before. My addiction to pornography began in part because I made a bad decision, or perhaps a series of bad decisions, that I never should have made. Everyone makes bad decisions in their lifetime, and most people recover from those decisions and move on. I did not. Most people can look at pornography without becoming addicted. I could not. Soon I was spending all that time I spent in hotel rooms looking at pornography. I could not stop. I used the high I received from sex and pornography to help me cope with life and keep from being overwhelmed by feelings I could not deal with. My series of bad decisions had led to addiction.

It was not long before I spent most of the little time I was at home doing the same thing. I would come home and isolate myself upstairs in my office, away from my family and any disruptions, staring at pornography on my computer monitor, trading images by email with others hooked by the same attraction. Hour after hour, I sometimes stayed upstairs until the wee hours of the morning. Nothing else seemed important. I roamed the darkest corners of the internet. I knew what I was doing was wrong, but I could not stop. Were my actions due to self-will? Or was something beyond self-will dragging me downward?

I have already told you about the day when a man in an internet chat room asked me if I had any pictures. I had responded, "No, send me some." He did, and I was on my way. When someone asked for pictures, I sent them. When I asked for pictures in return, I received them. It will sound strange, perhaps unbelievable, to those not addicted to pornography, but after a while pictures of naked people, even beautiful naked people engaged in sexual activities, all look the same. What most people would find crude, offensive, and immoral, I began to find boring. Soon I was seeking the different, the exotic, and eventually the illegal. The path for the different may go from fetishes to bondage, to bestiality, and eventually lead to the one place worse than all others —children.

The question came to me through an instant message that said, "Do you have any young?" I knew he was not asking for young adults. Of course, I said "No." I was horrified. Apparently, that made no difference. It was not long before I said, "No, send me some." And he did. I had stepped from a path I could rationalize as "Everybody's doing it" to the unthinkable: pornographic pictures of children. Some say that when a child is significantly abused, part of him is emotionally frozen at that age. Was I looking at fifteen-year-old children because I became emotionally frozen as a self-centered teenager who had not recovered from the abuse in the high school shower? Perhaps.

The addiction worked on me like a drug that only more pornography could satisfy. Justifying my behavior, I lost my judgment about any consequences of my behavior, including the damage I was causing myself and others. The compulsion spread and was out of control. I was an addict, caught in the cycle of shame, obsession, ritual, and compulsion. The addictive behavior was devastating to my self-image, as engaging in activities that I knew were wrong filled me with self-loathing. Caught in a circular process, I acted out again to quell the shame and self-loathing that was created by the acting out, creating more shame and self-loathing. Addiction became a prison from which I could not escape.

Soon I discovered there were a large number of people on the Internet desiring anonymous sex. There were personal ads, chat rooms, and websites devoted to procuring it for free. Just like twenty years before, I found myself meeting with strangers for sexual activity, but now in hotel rooms, homes, or sex clubs. I went into neighborhoods at night that before I would have avoided in the daytime. The damage I was doing to my family was buried beneath my compulsive biological urge for pornography and anonymous sex. I had an inexhaustible and limitless need to be desired. Although I knew what I was doing was wrong, I could not stop.

Once my addiction resurfaced, my life quickly spun out of control. I wanted to be in control of my life, so I shrank my nonaddictive activities down until they were small enough that I could feel in control. But the addiction had become my priority. Even my smallest decision was soon influenced by my need for sex and pornography.

When traveling, I would hurry back to the computer in my hotel room rather than socialize after a meeting. In my hotel room, I would decide to look at pornography rather than go to a nice restaurant for a meal, and then go out for a sexual liaison with someone I had never met. At home, I would stay upstairs on my computer rather than come down and watch TV with Ellyn. Two of our boys were married and lived in another state; the other was away from home in college. Ellyn felt alone and isolated. I would leave the computer to go to bed at two, three or four a.m. Although I did not realize it, I was powerless over my addiction.

My addiction had become a way of avoiding intimate contact, whether that contact was with my job and my superiors at the office, with friends, or with my wife and family. It had become an outlet to avoid life and emotional contact with others. My life had become unmanageable. I should have asked for help, but I was too ashamed. My only relief for my escalating desperation seemed to be to act out again.

Denial and rationalization are unconscious processes that all of us use at times to deal with our own imperfections. They are not intentional processes. But eventually denial turns into lying, which I consciously used to not get caught, to deceive my wife and children, my employer, and my friends. I became deviously manipulative and self-centered. Lying came easily to me and was easily accepted. I tried to stop lying, but I was unable to. I was afraid of discovery, of loss of control, of consequences. The lying destroyed what integrity and honor I had left. My self-esteem was gone.

Ellyn was unaware of my addiction to pornography and anonymous sex, but she knew something was wrong because she could see the ritual. I would come home from work, ask her how long it was until dinner, and disappear upstairs to my computer. Even there, my behavior had a very distinct but unchanging pattern: the way I turned on the computer, the sites I visited first, the order I opened email, the way I downloaded and hid the pornography. No thinking was involved; nothing interfered with the obsession.

There I was, a successful executive, a prominent man well known in my community and nationwide, a leader in my church, a man considered to be ethical and honorable, and a good citizen of high integrity, leading a double life. What a disparity there was between the person I presented to the public and my other self, the guy sitting at the computer ogling pictures of children engaging in sexual activity. I rationalized that I was only looking at pictures. I denied that I was hurting anyone. After all, I did not take the pictures; I did not purchase the pictures. The pictures were given to me by others who sent them in emails. I sent them on to others who wanted them. The fact that the children in those pictures were being abused, and that by viewing them I was contributing to that abuse, was not part of my abusive, dysfunctional thinking. I was a sex addict.

Did I realize that I would be caught? Others were caught, but I denied that it would happen to me. I prayed that if I were caught there would be no negative consequences to my family, my church, or my employer. I was kidding myself. I engaged in conflicted, broken thinking that makes no sense to anyone but an addict. But it made sense in my addicted mind. Today, those in my audience who are not addicts may find it very difficult to understand that I could think as I was thinking. An audience of recovering addicts understands and nods.

What Happened

CHAPTER 13

Caught

THE SEARCH

ON TUESDAY, MARCH 10, 2004, at 7:25 in the morning, I was given one of the greatest gifts I have ever received. I was given the gift of desperation. It did not seem like a gift at the time.

I had returned two days before from Washington, DC. I had been participating in a meeting at a major national organization dedicated to protecting children from sexual abuse. We were attempting to strengthen policies to protect children in schools. The meeting ended on Friday, but I had stayed in Washington until Sunday. I rationalized I was saving my employer money on airfare by taking advantage of the airline's policy of having lower airfares for those who stay over Saturday night. It was true I saved a few dollars, but that was not the reason I stayed. I stayed to have hours alone to look at the pornography on my computer and to visit a club in the most dangerous area of Washington. I was living a compartmentalized life, living the life of the self-righteous educator, husband, father, and Christian, while simultaneously living the life of the sex addict. The values I practiced in those two lives were diametrically opposed.

On Tuesday morning I awoke and got dressed and ready for work, just like I did on any other weekday morning. Ellyn was still in her nightgown and bathrobe. A few minutes before I was planning to leave the house there was a loud pounding on the door. "POLICE, OPEN UP!" I knew instantly that my life was about to become completely different. My worst nightmare had arrived, and I knew why they were there.

A dozen armed FBI agents poured through the front door and into our home. Ellyn backed away in alarm. "What are they looking for?" she asked, wide-eyed with fear and confusion. "Do they think we're hiding wanted criminals?" The officers ran from room to room checking for other people, shouting, "CLEAR! CLEAR! CLEAR!" Eventually the lead officer took me into my home office, closed the door, and handed me a search warrant. They were looking for child pornography.

I privately told Ellyn why the agents were there, and that they would find what they were looking for. I was in a stupor, moving from one unbelievable event to another. Ellyn was in complete shock. She was discovering a part of her husband that she had forgotten was there.

After I told Ellyn the truth about why the police were at the house, I called my assistant, Myra, at my office. I told her that I would not be in. I did not realize the FBI was already searching my office. An hour later I received a call from my boss, Mark. I had been placed on leave and was not to come to work or make any business contacts until he told me that I could. I knew that time would never come.

The search began upstairs in the bedroom where I kept my computer. They opened every box, checked every computer disk. There was very little pornography stored on my computer, and only one disk with a two- or three-minute video that was stored in a desk drawer. In a cabinet in the bedroom, however, hidden behind boxes and binders of old business correspondence was a small, locked, plastic storage box with old computer disks. I had not opened that box in five years, but I knew those disks contained hundreds of incriminating images. I knew when the FBI arrived at the door that they would find evidence of my illegal behavior, and when they brought down that plastic box, I knew I was in serious trouble.

The search continued for five hours. The agents left a list of those items they had confiscated, including three computers, computer disks, two cameras, a printer, financial records, and my passport. They were very professional. Once they departed, Ellyn and I were left alone in deafening silence to deal with the consequences of my self-destruction.

The Blur

Ellyn was distraught. Even though I had denied to myself the possibility of being caught, I had known that my behavior was illegal. Ellyn was caught completely by surprise. She too knew that life was about to be completely different, but she had no idea what to do or what would happen next. Her husband was not the man she had known for thirty-seven years. Feeling lost and afraid, she called the pastor of our church. They agreed to meet at a park because Ellyn was afraid to be seen at the church, where others could see that she had been crying.

I felt numb. My job was gone, my marriage in trouble. I did not know anyone who had been incarcerated, and I understood that I would be going to prison. I was suddenly forced to see the reality of my double life instead of the false image I had allowed people to see. I had violated every value I held dear in my life, and my wife, my boss, and my coworkers now knew of my hypocrisy. This was the lowest point of my life. I had hit bottom.

It was no doubt the lowest point in Ellyn's life too. How do you accurately describe a woman's love for her husband? Ellyn's loyalty to me is clearly shown by what happened next. In all the turmoil of my admission that I had been engaging in illegal and immoral behavior, lying to her, and the police searching the house, Ellyn's first concern was for me. She met our pastor in the park as planned, but Ellyn told him "I've left Brady alone. We have to go to the house." And they did.

The rest of the day was a blur. The pastor stayed and talked with us for a while. I called my two oldest children. Then I went to visit my son, whose college was not far away. They were shocked, but they all said the same thing. "I love you, Dad."

I knew many attorneys; none of them were defense attorneys. One of the elders at our church, Nathan, was a civil attorney who I respected. I was not excited about sharing my situation with Nathan, but I drove to his home. Nathan listened like the gentleman he was and said simply, "This is about the rest of your life. You need the very best attorney there is." He wrote a name and a phone number on a scrap of paper and handed it to me.

The Attorney Takes the Lead

Wayne McCallum was exactly the attorney I needed. We met on Thursday morning and found we had a lot in common. We both enjoyed nature and had similar experiences hiking, canoeing, and scuba diving. We were born on the same day, two years apart. Our oldest sons were born on the same day. A former prosecutor, Wayne was a leader in the state bar association. He knew everyone in the legal community and was well respected. He saw me as a good man who made a mistake. I saw him as an attorney I could trust.

I shared with Wayne that I was guilty and that I believed the prosecutor had the evidence he needed to convict me. On Monday we met with the lead FBI agent. I agreed to be interviewed and to answer all his questions. They agreed that nothing I said could be used against me. Wayne and I met at the FBI office with two agents in a closet-sized room. Everything I said was recorded and videotaped. I was advised to relax and tell the truth. The agents asked for my passwords and permission to use my screen name and pretend they were me. No promises were made that I would benefit from cooperating, but I hoped that would be the case. The interview lasted four hours.

At the end of interview, one of the agents said that I looked as if a massive weight had been lifted off my shoulders. I felt that way too. We pay a huge emotional price for keeping secrets. Jeffery Deaver describes in his novel *Cold Moon*:

> Whether you're deceptive to the cops or your mother or your husband or friends or yourself, the symptoms are always the same. You're stressed, angry, depressed. Lies turn people ugly. The truth does the opposite… Of course, sometimes it seems like the truth is the last thing you want. But I can't tell you how many times I've gotten a suspect to confess and he gives me this look, it's more like relief in his face. The weirdest thing: Sometimes they even say thanks.

I said "thanks." In a situation where I expected to be tense, I could feel the anxiety being lifted as I admitted my shameful behavior. With telling the truth, my recovery had begun.

The next step for me was a polygraph exam. Throughout history, those responsible for enforcing the law have attempted to develop lie detectors. One interrogation method used in Asia was based on the principle that salivation decreases during nervous tension. The mouths of several suspects were filled with rice, and the suspect with the greatest ease in spitting out the rice was judged guilty. The polygraph used today measures blood pressure, heart rate, respiration, and galvanic skin response, an increase in electrical conductance in the skin. The polygraph is controversial among psychologists and is wrong as often as 25% of the time, often detecting lies when the subject is being truthful. "Volunteering" to take the polygraph was a condition of my temporarily staying out of prison. So, I "volunteered."

The polygraph is subject to widespread limitations, but is still used extensively to scare the accused and those on probation into being truthful. Although I was clearly guilty of possessing child pornography, I had not been arrested and was not in custody. The information I revealed in the polygraph exam could be used against me. The primary purpose of this polygraph was to assure that I was not engaging in sexual relations with children. I was not, but the polygraph exam scared me a lot.

My expectations about what was about to happen were not even close to what actually happened. I was told that the examiner would ask me a series of questions. My attorney and an FBI agent were in the next room listening. The examiner would tell me the questions first, before I was attached to the polygraph, and I was to answer the questions. He repeated my name; I told him that was correct. He told me my address; I responded yes, that was my address. The next question was, "Do you have any secrets you don't want others to know?" I answered, "Of course." The examiner said, "Tell them to me." I did. Two grueling hours later – it seemed like more – I was attached to the polygraph for the first time. He asked if I was Brady C. I said "Yes." He repeated my address. I said "Yes." He asked if I had any secrets that I didn't want anyone to know, other than the ones I had told him. I said "No." He asked if I had ever touched a child's private parts (he was very specific). This was the real question. I said "No."

The agent said that the results of the exam were inconclusive. I was incredulous. I thought that wasn't possible. I had blabbed every sin I had ever committed. I spent another hour revealing secrets, this time secrets I was not even sure were accurate. Again, I was attached to the polygraph. I answered the same way. After four and a half hours, I was released. They finally believed I had told the truth.

There is no doubt the polygraph caused me to talk about things I had never discussed before. These were not things I was proud of, but they were not things I could be arrested for either. One thing was certain: I did not want to take a polygraph ever again. We do not always get what we want.

The Court and the Press

One of the worst parts of the legal process is the waiting. I no longer had a job and no longer had a computer. Time passed very slowly. Wayne and I had agreed that it was not necessary for the prosecutor to take my case to a grand jury; I was going to plead guilty without a grand jury indictment. The first hearing was set for six weeks to the day after the FBI came to my house. In the meantime, I waited and worried.

A few days before the hearing, Wayne and I went to the federal courthouse, where I was photographed and fingerprinted. I met with the pre-trial probation officer who would be responsible for my supervision until my sentencing. Until my sentencing I would be required to attend weekly group therapy. Anything I disclosed could be reported to my pre-trial officer and used against me at sentencing. Failure to cooperate would result in my immediate incarceration. I received permission to travel within the United States if I told my pre-trial officer where I would be and how to reach me. Although I was not in prison, I was no longer a free man.

Just when I thought things couldn't get any worse, they got worse. The day before my plea, Ellyn was out and I was home alone when the phone rang. The call was from NBC. The FBI public affairs office had sent a press release to the media. I told NBC to call Wayne and gave them his number. I immediately called Wayne. He said, "If they've called, it's already on MSNBC."

By 10:30 television crews appeared in front of the house. All the networks were there. I felt like a trapped rat. If I left the house, I'd be photographed and followed. I called Ellyn and warned her not to come home. The phone kept ringing – radio, TV stations, newspapers. My children called. The news media had found them at work. I did not turn on the TV or radio. I did not want to know what was said.

After a short break and the noon news, the TV reporters went door to door talking to my neighbors, who were shocked. The press learned nothing except that I was a good neighbor. I hoped the cameras would leave after the 5 p.m. news, but they did not. Members of our church offered to have us spend the night at their home, away from the media. I met Ellyn at the home of friends, terrified about my appearance in court the next day.

I suggested that Ellyn not go to the courthouse and avoid the emotional turmoil. I met Wayne at his office, reviewed what we expected to happen, and walked with him to the courthouse. I expected the press to be there; I did not expect the crowd of reporters and photographers waiting at the courthouse entrance. Wayne told the media that he would speak to them after the arraignment and that it was appropriate for the judge to hear my plea first. I said nothing and followed him into the courthouse, momentarily safe from the cameras that were not allowed inside.

Inside the courtroom, it was quiet; only two print reporters represented the media. Others present were employees of the court, defendants, and their lawyers. The three defendants, including myself, were called forward at the same time. I was dressed in a suit; the others were in the orange jumpsuits of inmates held in custody. The judge informed us of our rights, asked if our pleas were voluntary, and accepted guilty pleas from each of us. I was released on my own recognizance. The others were taken back into custody.

Wayne and I went to meet the press. He would speak to the press; I would walk back to his office. He believed the press would stay to hear what he had to say and leave me alone. He was wrong. When we got outside, the reporters split. Half would stay to hear Wayne tell them I was a good man who made a mistake; half followed me back to his office, cameras running. I said nothing, but was relieved when the door to Wayne's office closed behind me. Bad news travels fast. According to my son, who found the information on the Internet, the news of my guilty plea was covered in over two thousand reports on radio and TV stations, newspapers, and internet news. I felt humiliated.

FRIENDS

The next day Ellyn and I flew to be with one of our children, going into a supportive environment and away from the tension of being in a community where I was well known. Although I had been in the media there, nobody was expecting to see me, and I could relax with my family, unnoticed by anyone else.

We returned home a few days later to find a mailbox full of letters, sixty or seventy of them, from friends from all over the country who had seen us in the news. Two-thirds of the letters were addressed to both of us, expressing shock but offering support. Most of the rest were sent to Ellyn, from longtime friends recognizing her pain. The support for both of us was deeply appreciated.

One anonymous letter asked me to sign a petition to the Supreme Court asking that child pornography be legalized. Even when I was looking at child pornography every day, I knew that it was wrong and damaging. How could a man like me, who had dedicated his life to the education of children, to teaching them values, do the things that I did? Many recovering addicts wonder how they managed to make a wrong turn. Why did it happen and where? I didn't know, but I made a commitment to myself to find out.

I called my closest friends, people who thought they knew me well but from whom I had kept my closest secrets. I quickly found that several of them no longer wanted to talk to me. My behavior was not the behavior of the man they thought they knew. Emotionally the loss of these friendships was difficult.

Some people stand by you when the bottom seems to have fallen out of your world; others walk away. Only a few march toward you. My friend Carl was the first one to ask how he could help. He stored my hunting rifles in his attic until my children decided what to do with them. I would never again be allowed to use them. Bruce, whom I had known for over thirty-five years but with whom I had never been close, was retired and active in his church. He wrote me a simple letter: "We've known each other for a long time, and I've always considered you a friend. All I do now is drink coffee and play golf. If you want to do either of those things, call me." I did. Bruce was someone I could be honest with, offering me the kind of relationship I needed badly. We played golf, drank coffee, and talked. Bruce listened and did not judge. For a change, I was honest.

My childhood friend Joe and I maintained periodic contact. He had become an accomplished neurosurgeon. When he saw me on television, Joe called my attorney. He remembered the brain injury from hunting that I had as a fifteen-year-old. An old injury, which seemed to cause only inconsequential damage at the time can, as brain cells die away, cause unexpected damage. Brain damage, particularly to the frontal lobes, can bring out inappropriate behavior. People with no prior symptoms can suddenly begin shoplifting, shouting out in angry rage, exposing themselves, or become addicted to child pornography. Joe suggested an electroencephalograph (EEG) to detect abnormality in my brainwaves along with neuropsychological testing.

Our Church

More than anything else, Ellyn and I had three things in common: our children, the families of my coworkers, and our church. We had been active in our church for over eight years, both of us holding leadership roles when asked. We talked to the pastor about returning to church. He suggested that he call a meeting so I could talk with the congregation and they could discuss my continued participation. I agreed. The sanctuary was full that afternoon. I admitted my guilt, shared what had been happening, and asked their forgiveness. I acknowledged my very non-Christian behavior to a room full of Christian men and women, many of whom I had known for years. When I finished, Ellyn and I left them to discuss the problem of a known sinner in their midst.

The next Sunday Ellyn and I returned to church. We were among those who had been our friends. I had asked for forgiveness and was confident that

God had forgiven me. However, I could sense the discomfort in the congregation. Everyone sins, and God treats all sins equally. People do not.

That afternoon I was not surprised when the pastor called. Five families expressed that they were very uncomfortable that I was in church. He suggested that I not come to church for a couple of weeks while the congregation had a chance to think about their role as Christians. The pastor preached about forgiveness. Ellyn and I stayed home, away from the Christian support that we needed. Ellyn felt very angry. She was the victim of my behavior and the church's discomfort. She had not done anything wrong. I encouraged her to go to church, but she would not go without me. I recognized that I had committed a sin that is very difficult for people to forgive, and that the pastor was doing the best he could. However, nobody at the church called either Ellyn or me, and we became isolated. At the time in our life when we most needed Christian love, the support we needed from our church was limited. Several other churches invited us to attend, and we attended with friends who were members there. God reaches out in His own way.

The Pre-Sentence Investigation

Before sentencing, the probation department conducted a pre-sentence investigation. Wayne told me that this would be the worst part of the process, and it was. The department investigated all aspects of my life – family, education, work history, finances, drug and alcohol use, and any criminal background (I had none). Twice the officer interviewed me. The probation officer had all the information I had provided to the FBI agents, plus everything found in the search of our home. The report was mailed to both my home and Wayne's office. It recommended a sentence of 17 ½ to 20 years in prison. I was shocked and scared; 17 ½ to 20 years seemed excessive for looking at and exchanging photographs that, I rationalized, I did not take or purchase, images that were easily found on the Internet. If I had realized the importance of the pre-sentence report in determining my sentence, I would have been even more terrified.

I invited some friends to write the judge attesting to my otherwise good character and my contributions to the community. Many responded, and others heard about my request, called me, and offered to help. Many my friends from work wrote letters informing me that they had been told not to write. Even though the pre-sentence report is confidential, my former employer was afraid that the letters would be released and attract further negative publicity for them. Wayne wrote my employer's attorney, reminding him that instructing their employees not to write was obstruction of justice and against the law, but the employees had already been warned. Nonetheless, over 130 family and friends wrote the judge on my behalf. I am still extremely appreciative for their support.

My Addiction

> We are better at understanding morality than we are at living it. And that may be one of the great curses of mankind. I'm not aware of any other species that even has a moral sensibility. So we are blessed with having one, but cursed by our inability to abide by it.
>
> --New York Attorney General Elliot Spitzer, following his arrest for visiting high-priced prostitutes.

It was just a matter of time before the inevitable sentencing and prison. As an addict, my life had been in the control of forces that I did not understand. Now my life was in the control of a federal judge. I was very anxious.

Sex, which I had thought was a sacred value to me, had become depersonalized, and I had come to see my own deviant behavior as normal. My immediate task was to stop the addictive behavior. I had made that decision the morning the federal agents came to my house, after I was arrested but before I went into treatment. I knew the addictive pattern was encoded in my brain.

When Hurricane Andrew drew near Miami, where my mother then lived, the traffic heading north was bumper to bumper, stop and go. Thousands of people were driving away from the hurricane as it approached the metropolitan area. At that time, I was north of Miami and on the opposite coast in Tampa and wanted to check on my mother. I remember my surprise at being the only one on the road heading south. I think of this incident as a metaphor for my addiction. In my disease, it was as if I would always be heading into the eye of the storm. In situations where the sane flee from danger, I ran toward it, moving against the flow of everyday life, seeking the high of action and excitement, paying no attention to the dangers of my decision.

Often, I had risked my life, my reputation, and my relationships, by acting out in the hurricane of my sex addiction. I remembered the highs of my past behavior like the slow-motion replay of a football catch or the full moon slowly moving from horizon to horizon.

I gave up food, drink, sleep, and my own safety, my head filled with obsessions, ritually going through the motions, acting out again and again like the moth that seeks the candle flame with no regard for the heat. I had stopped my acting out behavior the morning the federal agents came to my house, but even after months of conscientiously doing things differently – not acting out sexually, not looking at pornography – old habits can return, as strong as before. Sometimes my past would come back at inconvenient times, such as at dinner with acquaintances or when I was reading a new book. Exposure to rewards, triggers, or emotional stressors can reactivate old patterns and drag the addict back into the addiction cycle.

The obsessions were still there, reminding me that relapse was a possibility. They frequently returned, particularly at bedtime and in the early morning. They were sometimes enjoyable. The addictive cycle continued to be embedded in my brain, waiting for an opportunity. The fear of my addiction returning was always with me. I was one slip, one poor decision away from relapsing into addictive behavior all over again.

Sex addiction is a massive violation of trust. I had broken trust with my wife and family, my employer, the youth pictured in the pornographic images I viewed, and the American public. Yet even when I found myself isolated, shameful, lonely, and even less satisfied than before after acting out, I had compulsively begun the cycle again. There came a time when I recognized I must reach out for professional help, as I could not manage life by myself.

Wayne had learned about a residential treatment center that specialized in helping people with sex addiction. We drove there and visited. I was impressed with the program and their presentation. They believed they could help me, and I felt good about what I heard. The location was beautiful and the attitude hopeful, but the price seemed astronomical. I would be there for at least three months. The relief I felt was mediated by worry about the cost.

I knew that I needed to change my life. Prison would change my location; I was not counting on prison for anything else. I had been humiliated by my arrest and even more by my actions that had brought about my arrest. Sex addiction had brought me the destruction of my self-esteem. I had been dishonest, immoral, and hostile. The Bible in 2 Peter, the second chapter, verse 15, says, "A man is a slave to whatever has mastered him." Sex addiction had mastered me. I needed help.

Some are dragged into treatment by their family, the courts, or professional licensing organizations. Some can look at themselves in the mirror, see something ugly, recognize it for what it is, and find a way to deal with it. I knew I had to begin healing and that I could not do it alone. Ellyn knew that I was going to prison and that we would be separated for a long time. Now I was volunteering for additional separation by seeking residential treatment. I was concerned too, but I knew that to heal my marriage I must first be healed myself.

CHAPTER 14

Into Treatment

KHALED HUSSEINI, IN HIS 2003 novel *The Kite Runner,* describes the situation of a young boy being brought from war torn Afghanistan to America as "lifting him from the certainty of turmoil to the turmoil of uncertainty." I was moving from the certain turmoil of sex addiction to the turmoil of uncertainty of treatment.

On arrival, I met with the psychiatrist who was the medical director of the treatment center. As we sat in his office, he explained that they were not only asking me to change my behavior, to stop acting out sexually, they were asking me to change my whole life. I had been acting as two people, one the husband, father, Christian, and employee that others saw; the other the hidden pornography and sex addict. Their goal was the fusion of those two identities into a single, balanced personality. It was terrifying to put my life into the hands of other people, but I knew I needed to face that terror and do just that.

The program was intensive, beginning with a period of group reflection at 7 a.m., involving programs all day long, and ending with a twelve-step recovery meeting every evening. For the first month I would be allowed to leave only for church on Sunday morning. As I earned privileges, I would be allowed to attend recovery meetings in the community. It would be months before I could drive to town for ice cream or a doughnut. Visiting was permitted only for a few hours on the weekends. There would be no smoking, no newspapers or television, no reading except recovery literature, no sex. Even masturbation was not permitted. I felt anxious but resolved. The next few months would be all about recovery.

The treatment center treated people with addictive behaviors: alcohol, drug, gambling, food, and sex addictions. They believed that all addictions had similar causes and that recovery came from similar treatment. I was introduced to the concept of compulsive sexual behavior as an addiction. Addiction is a pattern of thoughts, feelings, and behaviors that ensnare an individual, despite his knowing that those behaviors are damaging to himself (or herself) or others, and even though he knows the consequences. Addiction builds a prison of shame, despair, loneliness, and guilt that undermines his life and destroys a person's ability to be intimate with others or they with him. Addiction is not a problem of insufficient willpower, as many people think; rather, it's a chronic brain disease.

Many people believe that those who act out sexually are likely to continue doing so, and that treatment doesn't help. However, scientists now understand that these behaviors are treatable health issues. Many people recognize that alcoholism and drug addiction are also health issues. Gambling addiction and sex addiction both follow similar patterns to drug and alcohol addiction. Multiple lines of evidence indicate similar processes underlying all addictions, and most experts believe that addictions are not a collection of distinct disorders, but rather a disease with different manifestations.[vii] As with the alcoholic and drug addict, the sex addict acts out more than he intended, wants to cut back but is unable to do so, spends far more time engaged in obsessive thinking and addictive activity than he planned, continues his activity despite persistent social or psychological problems caused by the activity, acts out more and more to attain the same level of mood alteration, gives up other important activities to participate in his addiction, and suffers withdrawal cravings, anxiety, and depression when he is unable to act on his cravings.[viii]

The person who looks at pornography daily to relieve anxiety doesn't solve the real problem; he covers it up. What was sought as a solution becomes a problem. He fails to fill the hole inside him, and instead, makes the hole bigger. He avoids facing this problem by denying it, rationalizing it, and lying about it. He runs from conflict, from intimacy, and from feelings he is unable to handle. He is too ashamed. It is inevitable that eventually he runs back to the addiction. The rules that have governed his life since childhood, the rules that he learned from parents, church, and youth leaders, are overridden by the very different rules of the addict. When I heard this, I knew it described me.

Accepting that I had a disease was critical to my recovery. For me, knowing that I was ill reduced the shame I felt about my behavior. I am not proud of what I did, but this disease can be treated. I can have a future.

It is a deeply built-in part of human nature that we desire a partner with whom we can share tenderness, companionship, affection, and physical intimacy. Most adults do not seek intimacy by seeking sex with strangers in public parks or in the back rooms of XXX video stores, or by finding pictures of naked teenagers more erotic than those of adults, as I did. Others I met in treatment struggled with compulsions to wander through their neighborhood peeking in windows, or repeatedly fought off the temptation to inappropriately exhibit themselves in public places.

Experts today believe that these syndromes are diseases, and, as with cancer or diabetes, while it is not the person's fault he or she is ill, it nevertheless becomes his or her responsibility to take care of it. N. W. Galbreath in his 2002 article "Paraphilias and the Internet" wrote:

> When a person receives a diagnosis such as pedophilia, for example, it is important … to appreciate that it is not his fault that he has such a condition…No one would decide to be sexually oriented toward children. Rather, individuals discover that they are so afflicted. However, having in time made such a discovery, it becomes the individual's responsibility to do something about it so as to ensure that he will not cause problems in the lives of others.[ix]

I learned that human sexuality is not a simple process. Much of sexual behavior is the result of instinct and biology, rather than the result of choice[x]. Human sexual arousal is deeply imbedded in our behavior patterns. What arouses a person sexually is not always a voluntary decision.

We all do not have the same sexual drive. The sexual drive of some people may be propelled by a biological drive so powerful that an otherwise decent, law-abiding individual may, no matter how hard he or she attempts to do so, fail to resist sexual temptation. Where was I to find the power to overcome that temptation? That would be my most difficult challenge.

I had a deep desire to learn why I acted in the way I did. Causation of sexual pathology is not a simple issue. Many things can influence a person's brain: illegal drug use by the mother while she was pregnant, maternal stress caused by an abusive husband, low birth weight caused by premature birth. There may be a genetic predisposition to developing the disease, a biochemical imbalance in the brain, or an influence from the environment in which the individual grew up. Many developmental, social, and stressful life events may also help launch the illness. I needed to discover those issues in my life.

Early inappropriate sexual experiences or relationships, in particular, can contribute to inappropriate adult arousal patterns. Anecdotal evidence suggests that being a victim of child abuse is a strong predictor of becoming an abuser. I have personally heard many sex offenders tell stories of being sexually abused as innocent children. That was my story, too. One fellow patient was forcibly raped by his older brother from the time he was five years old until he was thirteen. As an adult, he searched the Internet for pornographic pictures of child rape until he was arrested for possession of child pornography and sought help.

Others report growing up in families where abuse occurred, and they were impacted, although they were not the victim. Witnessing violence or other trauma is also traumatic. One patient watched his father sexually abuse his brother. Jealous that he was not the one being abused (and the one receiving attention), he later abused his own children. In another situation, a young girl listened fearfully night after night to the sounds of her father raping her sister. As a thirty-six-year-old woman, she was arrested for sexually abusing her nine-year-old son. Although many abusers had early inappropriate experiences like the ones mentioned, most individuals who were victims do not become abusers.

My first roommate at the treatment center was Sam. Sam had a vivid memory of his father, again and again carrying Sam's younger sister, screaming, upstairs to rape her. Sam's mother sat in the other room, acting as if nothing was happening. As a boy Sam had learned to hate his father because of what he was doing to his sister; he wanted to help but was unable to do so. Fifty years later Sam, then a successful man at the pinnacle of his career, sexually abused his own granddaughter in much the same way. Sexual addiction was passed on through the lifelong memories of his father's actions. Memories became obsessions, the pattern became a ritual, and Sam began compulsively acting out in a way he had learned to hate as a child. Sam's story has a happier ending than most. Sam realized that turning himself in to the police was the only way his granddaughter could get the help she needed. He spent four months at a private treatment center for sex addiction and was incarcerated for a year and a half. His granddaughter received therapy, and Sam's family, damaged as it was, is together again.

Thirty-year-old Richard, a bisexual man, was raised in a home with a father, a prominent attorney, who was a perfectionist and often abused him physically during fits of rage. Even thinking of his father could bring Richard to the point of trembling fear, and he chose to move across the country to be away from his father. With therapy and participation in twelve-step programs, Richard was progressing well in his recovery from alcoholism, drug addiction, and compulsive anonymous sexual activity. He had not used alcohol or illegal drugs for almost a year when Richard's father called him, telling him he was planning to be in his city for business and wanted to visit. The fear of seeing his father triggered Richard to relapse. That same night Richard developed cravings to engage in sexual behavior with a young stranger. He found an eighteen- year-old college student he had never met on a website, and invited the student to his apartment for sexual activity, despite his constant pledges that he would never engage in this type of behavior again. Once the addiction was triggered he could not stop the cycle. I met Richard when he entered residential treatment one more time. In a strange way, it was a relief to learn that my experiences were not unique. I benefited from being with others who were also recovering from serious compulsive sexual illnesses.

I also learned that homosexual children are particularly vulnerable to parental and societal pressure to deny their natural sexual feelings, leading to self-doubt or self-hatred and an inability to develop appropriate adult arousal patterns. This dynamic of denial of sexuality, considered by some to be emotional abuse, may lead biologically predisposed individuals to developing deviant sexual behavior. The prohibition against homosexuality likely has contributed to the prevalence of sexual addiction in this country for gay, bisexual, and transgender people.[xi]

As I read and listened, I learned that early sexual fantasies may be a significant factor in the development of deviant patterns of arousal, particularly when the fantasies are reinforced by the powerful sexual euphoria that results from masturbation. In 1938, behavioral scientist B. F. Skinner published *The Behavior of Organisms,* in which he laid out the principles of operant conditioning, still relevant today. He established that behavior changes because of the consequences of that behavior. For example, the strong pleasure resulting from masturbation provides significant reinforcement for that behavior. Before an offender acts out in a deviant way, he may fantasize that behavior hundreds or even thousands of times while masturbating. Every additional recollection of a memory provides additional strength to the memory, making it easier to retrieve and more difficult to resist.

I learned that the causation of sexual disorders is a complex mix of biological, neurological, genetic, and learned behaviors. My sexual deviancy went well beyond simply making bad decisions; other powerful forces were involved. Understanding those forces in my life would make my recovery easier.

CHAPTER 15

Understanding Sexual Addiction

In 1642 seventeen-year-old Thomas Granger, a servant to an honest man in Duxbury, was convicted of having sexual relations with a mare, a cow, two goats, five sheep, two calves, and a turkey. He was executed on September 8, 1642, but not until the boy had witnessed the killing of his animal paramours, which were all buried in the same pit.

– Nathanial Hawthorn's *Mayflower* as quoted from the diary of William Bradford.

Three hundred fifty-five years later, William Jefferson Clinton, president of the world's most powerful nation, engaged in oral sex with a White House intern in a small hallway off the oval office, then lied about it. It was rumored that this was a regular, compulsive pattern of behavior.

In 2009, Tiger Woods, one of the wealthiest and most famous athletes of all time, entered treatment for sex addiction, admitting to multiple affairs.

Sex addiction has been around for a long time, and it can affect men and women of any income level or social status. Politicians, farmers, athletes, policemen, coaches, teachers, business executives, ministers, and Boy Scout leaders – all have sexually acted out in potentially shameful ways, violating their own personal values, yet unable to stop.

How does addiction begin? I was asked to read *Out of the Shadows* by Patrick Carnes, a pioneer in the field of sexual addiction. Carnes describes the development of delusional thought processes that are rooted in the addict's belief system. Working with sex addicts, he identified four basic core beliefs, self-judgments of the addict:

1. "I am basically a bad, unworthy person." The addict has low self-esteem and does not believe he (or she) is attractive physically or personally. He or she feels humiliated and inadequate. This belief creates a barrier between the addict and other people. Addicts hide the reality of their addiction because they feel ashamed and unworthy.
2. "No one would love me as I am." If anyone knew about the addict's secret addictive behavior he believes they would abandon him. He cannot express remorse or guilt or be honest about his behavior because he is afraid he will not be loved if the listener knew.
3. "My needs are never going to be met if I have to depend upon others." Addicts feel unable to trust or love anyone else. Consequently, they isolate, manipulate others, and depend only on themselves. Relationships don't work for them.
4. "Sex (or cocaine, alcohol, gambling, etc.) is my most important need." The addict confuses the addictive process or substance with support, care, or affirmation; ironically, it provides only an illusion of what he or she is seeking. The addiction seems to make the pain in the addict's life bearable and progressively becomes the priority in the addict's mind.[xii]

I could easily see that I also judged myself using those core beliefs. I knew what I was doing was wrong and condemned myself for my behavior. I was afraid to tell anyone about my actions because I was sure they would not love me if they knew. I did not trust anyone else and consequently could not ask for help. By my actions I put my addiction first, ahead of God, family, friends, my job, and even my freedom.

Addicts use distorted thinking to convince themselves that what they are doing is acceptable. Denial, minimizing the consequences of the destructive behaviors, blaming others, and ignoring the problem are on the list of thinking disorders. In time, the addict begins to believe his own flawed thinking. F. Lyles Arnold, who has been providing therapy to those with a history of deviant sexual behavior for twenty-five years, says:

> Thinking errors serve specific purposes. We utilize thinking errors in order to convince ourselves that it will be all right to do something we fundamentally know it is not all right to do. We use thinking errors to avoid responsibility when we are being held accountable for our actions. A person might use a thinking error in order to soothe his guilty conscience or to calm his fears after he has done something that he knows is wrong and that he could get in trouble for.

As the addict grows increasingly isolated from others, the feedback loops that ordinarily serve to correct impaired thinking are gone. Once the addiction takes hold, self-knowledge that would normally cause someone to question his behavior has been distorted and is no longer effective, perpetuating the damaged thinking and acting-out behavior.

Individuals use different ways to suppress uncomfortable emotions. Healthy individuals anchor their thinking in reality; addicts turn to an addictive substance or process such as alcohol, drugs, work, or gambling[xiii]. Many, like me, tend to engage in compulsive sexual behavior. I was struck by how close this fictional example of a gambler from Pearl Buck's classic 1932 novel *The Good Earth* was to the experience of the sex addict.

> Wang Lung had before this passed the place by, filled with the horror at the thought of how money was being spent there in gambling and in play and in evil women. But now, driven by his unrest from idleness and wishing to escape from the reproach of his own heart when he remembered that he had been unjust to his wife, he went toward this place. Thus he stepped across the threshold.

How many times does the sex addict step across the threshold to escape from the reproach of his own heart? Too many to count.

I learned that addictive patterns with alcohol, food, work, money, sex or romance, or other addictions substitute for relations with people; they offer immediate gratification, temporary modulation of mood and affect, and a sense of control over the process[xiv].

Life is full of events, people, places, and things that influence thoughts, emotions, and behaviors. The addictive cycle, like any behavioral cycle, may be activated by certain events. A man whose girlfriend dumps him would probably be sad or angry. A person working for a company that's reducing employment may be anxious. These are legitimate emotions, but in an addict they reinforce his or her core negative beliefs.

Someone addicted to anonymous sex may be triggered by accidentally driving by a park or other cruising spot. He may think about his experiences there, feel shame and then anxiety about those experiences, and begin obsessing about future possibilities. Seeing a former sex partner in a bar or restaurant can trigger a woman who engages in multiple affairs. An addict who walks into a convenience store that feels damp and smoky can be triggered by memories of the same smell in the back of a porn store. An open window can trigger a voyeur. A situation may trigger a certain thought or emotion that leads to the addictive cycle and compulsive behavior. We don't choose our triggers, they choose us. The addict engages in his or her addiction to relieve the feelings, triggering the addictive cycle. Once the cycle has been triggered, it is difficult to stop.

Once triggered, bringing about distorted thoughts, the trap of addiction occurs in four connected, repeating, and unending stages.

- Shame, Despair, Anxiety: The inability to process these uncomfortable emotions fuels the addictive cycle.
- Obsession: Unwanted thoughts and images enter the mind and block out the anxiety.
- Ritual: A series of acts are regularly repeated in a very similar way so as not to interfere with the obsession.
- Compulsion: The compulsive acting-out of behaviors damaging to self or others leads full circle to shame and despair, creating a continuous cycle.

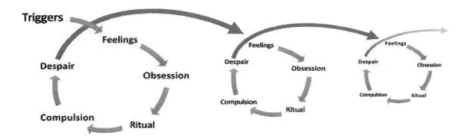

Here's how the cycle looked in my life:

Those engaging in compulsive behavior generally don't handle emotions well. The most dangerous emotions, and the ones that hold many in their addiction, are shame, resentment, fear, and despair. But what can the addict do with those emotions? Who can he tell he was using heroin or looking at child pornography? The addict believes he is a bad person. His actions were too shameful. Who can he tell that he exposed himself in the supermarket parking lot and thinks he may be been identified? No one would love him if they knew. He is too afraid and in despair. Who can she tell that she lost her life savings in a single drunken night in a casino? She can't tell anyone. She is afraid to trust anyone else. Her behavior, she thinks, cannot be forgiven. In a loop of unmanageability, the emotions that were created by the dysfunctional behavior become triggers for more dysfunctional behavior.

The addictive behavior has become the most important thing. The addict's core beliefs contain false assumptions that lead to distorted thinking; they isolate the addict from reality. This supports the addictive cycle, which in turn gives credence to the addict's core beliefs. The addict is caught in a whirlpool and does not know how to get out.

Addiction is one of several mental disorders in which obsessive thoughts overrun a person's mind and take over his or her life. As if the addict is in a trance, these thoughts occur over and over again and become absolutely automatic. The addict has no choice. The automaticity helps the addict think he is in control when, in fact, he is out of control.

The obsession prevents the painful memory from consciously continuing, but the immediate, short-term relief keeps self-defeating compulsions alive. So he begins an obsessive mental search that leads toward compulsive activity.

The obsession not only somewhat buries the shame of past and current activities, it buries concern for the love of his spouse and family, it progressively destroys his effectiveness at work, and it displaces concern for his friends. The search for the next experience, the high of a drug-filled night, the excitement of winning the jackpot on a slot machine, or the next secret sexual encounter in a public park, can be completely overwhelming. The fact that those behaviors are wrong and forbidden becomes smothered by the excitement and anticipation. The trap is set.

Steven, a dentist who became a friend in treatment, was married with three children. He had sixteen affairs with patients and employees in a one-year period, many of those affairs occurring concurrently. He obsessed daily about having an affair with beautiful patients. He could not stop until a complaint was made to the medical board and he was required to enter residential treatment.

Ritual is an attempt to control circumstances and feelings that would otherwise be overwhelming. Addiction creates ritual; that is, a repetitive way of doing things that bypasses thinking, allowing the addict to feel in control, even when he is becoming more and more out of control. The ritual may be the way a drug addict drives the same way to the drug house, always taking the identical route, or the way the alcoholic stops at the same bar on the way home from work every night, always sitting on the same stool and talking with the same bartender. It may be the way the sex addict wanders through the same park three times a week seeking illicit activity. Choosing familiar patterns allows the addict to feel in control of his decision-making, even when he is becoming more and more entrenched in his patterns, and less and less in control of his behavior.

Phillip, another patient, a business owner and the graduate of a major university, has been arrested seven times for voyeurism. He walked the same route through his neighborhood every night, seeking the enticing view of naked women through uncovered windows. He could not control his compulsive behavior. Now in recovery, Phillip breaks the ritual by not leaving his house at night unaccompanied.

The obsession and ritual have only one result: the inevitable compulsive behavior. The urge to act is stronger than the will to resist. As the ritual develops, the addict knows he is going to act out as certainly as the hunter knows that when he pulls the trigger he no longer has any decisions to make. The bullet is on its way.

Stuart, a 50-year-old married man, had been raised by an abusive father and carried his anger at him into adulthood. Stuart's ritual included drinking, going to second-hand stores and dressing like a street person, and then manipulating older men into sexual activity, temporarily relieving the anger he had at his father.

I could see how my addiction followed this same pattern. There was a direct relationship between the times my addiction was most active and increased stress at work or at home. The obsessions strengthened when I got on an airplane to travel. My mind was not focused on the business reasons for the travel; it was dreaming of acting out. I had a ritual related to how I used the computer. I did not go directly to pornography or chat rooms; I began in places that I thought were not dangerous and progressed through them in a similar order every time. My obsession and ritual almost always ended in acting out. I sought anonymous sex in my hotel room or someone's home. If I couldn't arrange that, I went to a XXX video store or sex club to find someone to hook up with. Pornography was my last choice, but I turned to pornography when other outlets were not available. But when I acted out, when the act was completed, I felt terrible. I knew what I was doing was wrong. I felt guilty, ashamed, and in despair. The only way to end those painful feelings was to act out again. So the cycle began again for me.

In summary, I could now see that my addiction was activated by certain events, called triggers. It was clear that I used compulsive behavior to suppress uncomfortable emotions; that is, emotions often triggered obsessions, rituals, and compulsions, sometimes outside my awareness. However, the compulsive behavior didn't meet my needs, and instead engendered shame, despair, and anxiety. Those emotions were so painful that I began sexual obsessions to relieve the pain, fueling the addictive cycle to begin again.

CHAPTER 16

You Too? I Thought I Was the Only One.

THERAPISTS KNOW THAT SHAME WORKS in secret and loses its power when it is exposed to the community. My first written assignment in therapy was to write my life story, completely and honestly, including my sexual history. When finished, I would share it with a group of fifteen other addicts. Writing my story took a month. At times my hand wouldn't move, and my pen wouldn't write. I would sit frozen, numb, at the desk in my unadorned room. I felt overwhelming shame. My story showed that my life had been out of control. As I began attending twelve-step meetings, I learned Step 1: "**We admitted we were powerless over our sexual addiction – that our lives had become unmanageable.**" [1] As I wrote, I could see the compulsiveness of my behaviors and the self-centeredness that had consumed my life. I could identify thoughts, feelings, and situations that were triggers to my behavior; obsessions that filled my mind; and behavioral rituals that paved the way to my compulsive sexual behavior. I saw that I fled from intimacy and real friendships, and the way I avoided conflict rather than face it. I saw my lack of a true relationship with God.

When I finished writing my life story, I spent two hours reading it to the group. I quickly learned that you can't fool another recovering addict. They have been where you have been. They asked tough questions, but were satisfied with my answers. The group of addicts voted to accept my story.

---

1 I chose to use the steps from the book *Sex Addicts Anonymous* (International Service Organization of SAA, Inc, 2005). The steps from the book *Sexaholics Anonymous* (Sexaholics Anonymous, 1989) are similar, and I have no personal preference.

Once again, revealing secrets removed some of the weight I could feel on my shoulders.

I had lived life in a world where individuality and self-sufficiency were paramount. I learned that in difficult times I could count on me. This time I could not. This disease, this addiction, had a power over me that caused me to act against my own will. I could not change myself on my own; my individual will-power was not enough. The emotional cues that I came to know as triggers overpowered my conscious intention. I oscillated between indulging myself and then, full of shame, restricting myself. I was told that the answer was the opposite of what I had spent a lifetime learning. Surrender. Give up indulging and give up restraining. Let go. Admit that I could not do this on my own. If I was not powerful enough to control my addiction, then I needed to find a power greater than myself.

That led to Step Two: **"Came to believe that a power greater than ourselves could restore us to sanity."**

Most addiction recovery programs primarily use group work. When I was placed in a group of other addicts who suffered from similar problems, who had been where I had been, and like me, were trying to recover, the shame lifted. The gift of twelve-step recovery programs is that people really care that you are there, and they show it. As fellow addicts, we accepted and supported each other as equals. We did not judge each other. C. S. Lewis wrote that real friendship begins in the moment when a person says "What! You too? I thought I was the only one." I was not alone. As other addicts shared their stories, their experience, and their strength and hope, I heard my own story. Hearing about their recovery gave me hope for mine, and I began to see the possibility of an addiction-free future. In the beginning I saw the group as my Higher Power and turned my life over to the group.

Dealing with Trauma

Legendary neurologist Sigmund Freud believed that a patient's buried traumatic experiences could be the underlying cause of their behavior problems. He believed those traumatic experiences could be repressed, hidden from the conscious mind. For the patient to recover, the buried experiences need to be brought to the level of consciousness and their power removed from them. Since Freud, mental health professionals have generally acknowledged the importance of accessing traumatic emotional experiences in order to integrate and release the buried emotions; correct negative assumptions formed from the trauma; and develop healthier, more realistic beliefs about oneself and others. Modern-day researchers and theorists have confirmed that addiction is often in part caused by traumatic experiences of abuse or neglect that occurred in childhood[xv]. Reviewing my childhood to identify and resolve my buried traumatic experiences was helpful, and perhaps essential, to my recovery.

Those who come through childhood trauma into adulthood develop elaborate ways to handle the pain of trauma, and they often deny it completely. They cover up the painful thoughts and emotions and they deny the harm done by parents and others. They mask their fear with denial and their lack of self-worth with perfectionism, and they carry these defense mechanisms that were necessary as children into adulthood, where they become damaging and debilitating. Until the childhood trauma is examined, along with the effects of the trauma on their self-image and relationships are examined, they are unlikely to repair the damage.

EMDR

Dr. Francine Shapiro noticed when walking through a park that disturbing thoughts she had been having were disappearing. She realized that when a disturbing thought arose her eyes began to move rapidly, which seemed to help the thought to leave her consciousness. When the thought resurfaced, it seemed to have lost most of its negative charge. From that experience she developed a program called Eye Movement Desensitization and Reprocessing (EMDR).

In an EMDR therapy session, a patient is asked to access memories, thoughts, and feelings related to a traumatic event and discuss them with the therapist. As the patient speaks, a pencil or a light is moved from side to side in front of the person's eyes, or metronome-type sounds are repeated from ear to ear. When the patient talks with the therapist again about the traumatic memories, they usually have lost their power. Theoretically, the emotional affect, or charge, has been either released or integrated into healthier brain functioning. The affect having dissipated, the defense mechanisms become unnecessary. The memory remains, but without the devastating effects[xvi] (Parnell, 2007, pp. 18-19).

My therapist, Anne, worked with me at the treatment center. With EMDR I was able to access memories of traumatic events and re-experience as an adult what I had experienced as a child. To me the most dramatic event was the abuse I endured in the high school shower. When we accessed those memories, I could clearly see myself, a small naked boy, being brutally abused.

Every day at the center, during my free time, I walked wooded trails through the property, thinking. Anne suggested that I take the abused boy with me when I walk and reassure him that he had grown up and I was safe now. I felt strange walking with an invisible child, as if I was insane. However, I did as I was told, and in time I could feel the power of that abuse slowly disappearing.

I also accessed memories of events in my family, often finding that the memories I accessed were quite different from those I had consciously remembered. But my anger remained. Eventually I came to recognize that my parents had their own stories, experiences in their lives that were beyond my understanding and perhaps theirs. Just as my life experiences were based on actions from my childhood, so were the actions of my parents based on experiences from their childhood. They were imperfect people who made mistakes. In time, I came to understand that my parents did the best they could. This, in turn, allowed for compassion and forgiveness. But this process took a very long time.

Psychological Immaturity

I learned about the ways childhood trauma influenced my behavior and led me toward addiction. Toni, a talented therapist, taught me theories of codependency. One type of childhood trauma results from immature parenting, albeit usually unconscious and unintentional. That trauma comes from abuse, neglect, abandonment, and the expectation that the child should fill needs of the parents, rather than the other way around.

As the therapist drew this on a whiteboard, I could see the effects of my family's dysfunctional dynamics on my life. These behavior patterns caused anger, fear, shame, guilt, sadness, and loneliness, and made my childhood very painful. They led to immaturity as a child and detrimental behaviors as an adult.

In her book *Facing Codependence*[xvii], Pia Mellody, a nationally recognized expert in codependence and addiction, has suggested that developmental immaturity shows itself through five core areas: self-esteem, boundaries, reality, wants and needs, and moderation of emotions.

- The child has developed self-esteem based on the attention he received from others rather than his own internal value, and feels either worthless or, to compensate, arrogant and grandiose.
- He or she either develops rigid boundaries or functions without clear boundaries. With overly rigid boundaries we become isolated from others. Without clear boundaries we have no limits; we lose our way or don't know how to say no. We either use people or let ourselves be used.
- Rather than accepting that it's normal to be imperfect, the child either accepts someone else's perfectionist reality or accepts no reality at all. Many people have difficulty owning the reality of their thoughts, their emotions, their appearance, or their behavior.
- Rather than experiencing normal interdependence with others, the child becomes either numb to internal wants and needs or overwhelmed with neediness and overly dependent.
- Rather than developing spontaneous and modulated access to and expression of the emotions of childhood, he or she feels either emotionally numb, or hysterical and full of feelings, such as anger, fear, sadness, and shame.

These symptoms carry over into adulthood, where they become dysfunctional and painful. To mediate the pain that results from not appropriately expressing emotions, the adult often resorts to addictive behavior: alcohol, drugs, nicotine, eating disorders, codependence, work addiction, sex, gambling, or others. As I looked back at my own childhood, I saw I had struggled with self-esteem and boundaries. I denied my own thoughts, needs, feelings, and behavior. I did not express my emotions, keeping them bottled up. I did not recognize my own needs and would not ask for help. My needs continued to exist, and while outwardly I lived as a perfectionist as an attempt to maintain control, inwardly I indulged in need gratification in distorted, inappropriate ways.

Recovery begins with pain. As I recovered, I would need to confront the symptoms. I needed to rebuild my self-esteem, develop an ability to be intimate, become able to accept my imperfections, accept responsibility for my decisions, be able to experience reality moderately, and learn to ask for help from God and others. This transformation was daunting.

Our feelings are produced from the way we interpret what is going on around us. I learned that my thinking about the world around me had been damaged by the abuse that occurred in my childhood. I had been unable to express or even recognize my feelings. This liability became a significant barrier as I sought intimate relationships. To deal with an emotion, it is first necessary to recognize that we feel it. Only then can we learn to express it properly. When I didn't properly recognize how I felt, the conclusions I drew from events were frequently inaccurate and I didn't realize it. As I held in anger, it had turned to the type of self-righteousness that allowed me to look at child pornography without feeling the horror that most people would feel.

In treatment, there was a daily emphasis on learning how to feel. As I described my addictive behavior, I was asked, "How did you feel?" Often, I didn't feel anything. I was numb. How should I have felt? I should have felt ashamed. However, I already believed that I was inherently inferior. The shame was already there; it was the root of my addiction. Only as I learned to recognize my emotions would I begin to recover. I had to force myself to think about how I was feeling on a regular basis.

SPIRITUALITY

I had been a Christian all my life. As a child I was baptized, had years of perfect attendance at Sunday School, and was confirmed as a member of the church. Ellyn and I attended church regularly. I held major leadership positions in every church we attended. Yet all my Christian beliefs and activities failed to inhibit my addictive behaviors. I asked God many times to take away my addiction to pornography and sexual infidelity, but I did not see any change. One of the annoying things about God is that He seldom gives us just what we think we want. God has his own way of testing us and showing us what's important. It was only after I began to understand God's expectations of me and began to do my part that He helped me into recovery.

The spiritual feelings that I needed did not arise, for me, from going to church or reading the Bible. Those helped, of course. But my spirituality arose out of the shame that reminded me that I needed a God more powerful than I was. It came from my most private inner experiences that insisted there was a larger meaning to life, and that meaning came from God. As a self-reliant human being, I had become my own god. As an addict, sex became my god. In recovery I was told I needed to remember two things: "There is a God. You're not Him." If I was powerless over my addiction and my life was unmanageable, if I could not recover on my own, but others like me did recover, then there must be another way. I had been praying for the wrong thing and praying from my diseased point of view, rather than God's.

I was at Step 3. **"Made a decision to turn our will and our lives over to the care of God, as we understood God."**

I fell to my knees and prayed in desperate hope, and the greatest sincerity I had ever had in my life, the third-step prayer from the Big Book of Alcoholics Anonymous:

God, I offer myself to Thee – to build with me and do with me as Thou wilt.
Relieve me of the bondage of self, that I may better do Thy will.
Take away my difficulties, that victory over them may bear witness to those

I would help of Thy Power, Thy Love, and Thy Way of Life.
May I do Thy will always!^{xviii}

I felt a great peace and serenity come over me. I didn't know what to do next, but I trusted that knowledge would come in time.

Today I am reminded of the story of three birds sitting on a fence. One made a decision to fly away. How many were left? Three were left. The one had only made a decision. The hard work was ahead.

I began regular prayer and meditation. I took action to develop a relationship with God unlike any I had had before. God had been with me all along. I was the one who had failed to turn my life over to Him. It was time for me to do what God wanted, not what Brady wanted. That would not happen instantly.

CHAPTER 17

I'm Not Much, But I'm All I Think About

CONFESSION

IN ADDICTION MY FACE WAS turned to the past: resentments from long ago, anger at those who had treated me poorly, blaming my problems on what someone else had done. I would like to do things over, but I cannot. Miguel Syjuco states in his 2010 novel, *Illustrado*:

> If only we could go back and reverse the things we did wrong, better the things we did right. We can't. Not because time doesn't move that way, but because we ourselves would be entirely different. It would not be fair. You've had your chance. You are no longer on the stage. The trumpets are silent, packed up in cases gathering dust.

At the treatment center, they said it differently: "You can't un-ring a bell." I could not change my past, but I had to deal with it. A friend in recovery, Bill, refers to the past as a heavy backpack that we carry around, weighing us down. Only when we deal with the resentments, anger, and blame, only when we seek out the defects in our own character, can we begin to put the past behind us.

Was I, a child raised in a home that placed blame and engendered shame, missing things that I should have learned but never did, led to addiction by my past? Did the experiences of my life influence my vulnerability to stress and send me onto the addiction trail? My mother's perfectionism and bitter criticism came back to me repeatedly, like a splinter that continually works its way to the surface. But living with resentment is like taking poison and expecting the other person to die. The poison ate at me from the inside. My own anger and hatred came back and attacked me, and I was the one being harmed by my own resentments. It was time for me to accept responsibility. I needed to inventory my own life and accept my own sins.

The stories of men who descended into alcoholism or addiction because of regrets of the loss of a girlfriend or the tragic results of an accident are part of the American fabric. For many, as we look back on our life history, the regrets stand out more prominently than the positive memories, haunting us until we resolve them.

When I resented things that happened to me and blamed others, I became a victim. Living in bitterness was like being handcuffed to the person who wounded me, as I had become dependent on them to change. For those events that happened when I was a child, I learned to actively forgive those involved. For those things that occurred when I was an adult, in order to recover I needed to accept the truth of what happened, and clarify my part. Ellyn's vulnerability to depression came from her own childhood. But my actions toward her were harmful. When I called home and heard her depressed voice, instead of expressing compassion, I would work more hours or bury myself in pornography.

The boss had the right to determine the direction of the corporation. I had a commitment to change that he did not share. When I failed to influence company decisions to my own satisfaction, I could have quit and gone to work for someone else. I did not. For me to recover from addiction, no one else has to change. I do. Every day I use the Serenity Prayer to ask God to give me the serenity to accept the things I cannot change, and I have come to realize that is almost everything. I am powerless to change the weather, the traffic, my boss, or my wife's depression. Then I ask God for the courage to change the things I can and for the wisdom to know the difference. It took me awhile to recognize that almost the only thing I could change was me and my attitude. What a surprise it was, that when I changed my attitude, my wife's depression almost disappeared.

I began to write about what happened to me and who else was involved. I also began to realize what I could do to untie myself from my past abuse.

I could change whether the offender changed or not. I needed to accept my own limitations and those of others. In identifying my own part in my difficulties, I let go of my resentments toward others, and in their place I developed compassion and forgiveness.

The fourth step of twelve step recovery programs reads: **"Made a searching and fearless moral inventory of ourselves."** Twelve-step groups such as Sexaholics Anonymous and Sex Addicts Anonymous ask their participants to become aware of their character defects by listing them. I did this, and my list was lengthy. Self-centeredness led the list. Everything I did as an addict revolved around me. Recovery friend Earl put it this way: "I'm not much, but I'm all I think about." In my addiction, I did not think of the abuse being perpetrated on the youth being pictured. I did not think about the damage I did to Ellyn or my children when I was not present, physically or emotionally, to help them. I did not think about the damage to my employer when I was obsessing about pornography rather than thinking about my job. My wife, my children, and my employer would all be hurt when I was arrested, but I didn't think about that either. All I thought about was my selfish gratification of my addiction.

Super-achievement and perfectionism are two characteristics that arose from the unreasonable expectations of my childhood. I discovered that my drive for achievement was an attempt to compensate for my childhood failures on the athletic field and my inability to satisfy my parents. It emerged as a drive that put work first and everything else second. I had a hunger to be successful, and that success fed my ego. At the same time, the hours I spent at work helped to conceal the seemingly bottomless loneliness, anger, and shame that I carried within me. When work no longer was satisfying, when it no longer concealed my childhood trauma, I needed to go somewhere else. I went to pornography and sex.

Perfectionism led to feelings of grandiosity. If I thought of myself as perfect, then everyone else was less than perfect. It led me to feel that I was in control, that my will was correct. One of the problems with perfectionism is that it demands failure. When I failed to meet my own unrealistic standards of perfection, my ego was dashed again; I blamed others or foolishly continued to insist that I was correct, as if the blue sky was orange simply because I said it was. Perfectionism was also a barrier to seeking help. If I am perfect, I don't need help. My perfectionism was not that grossly open, at least not to me. When my therapist handed me an article on perfectionism, I responded, "You think I'm a perfectionist?" I was, and I was blind to my own imperfections.

Dishonesty is an inherent part of addiction. As an addict, I had to lie and manipulate others. I was too ashamed to be honest. My perfectionism would not allow me to be honest about my own defects. If anyone else knew that I was looking at child pornography, they would judge me and be unable to forgive me. Lying also allowed me to stay in control. By lying, I could continue my addictive behavior. I lied about what I was looking at on the computer. I lied about what it was that kept me so busy on business trips that I didn't find time to call home. Recovery professionals say that addiction is the disease that makes you think you do not have it. I believed my own lies.

Another problem with secrets is that keeping them is unhealthy for the brain. Psychologist James Pennebaker studied rape and incest victims who chose to keep their victimization secret. Pennebaker concluded that not discussing the event might have been more damaging than the event itself. But the secret loses its power when you talk about it. When subjects disclosed their secrets, their health improved, they needed to see their doctors less often, and they had a measurable reduction in stress[xix]. I knew I had to become rigorously honest.

By assessing my weaknesses, I was figuring out the things that brought about my addiction. Sex was not on the list. I identified those things that triggered my cravings for sex and pornography – regrets and resentments, feeling like a victim, self-centeredness, perfectionism, and excessive need for achievement – and those things that kept me in addiction, like dishonesty. I examined those things that I feared, and those people I had hurt, sexually and otherwise. I admitted these defects, every one of them, to myself and to a friend in recovery (my sponsor). I asked God to help me remove these defects in my character, to take away the fear, to heal the resentments. God works in his own time, but I knew He was helping me to recover.

CHAPTER 18

Family Therapy

ADDICTION DESTROYS MARRIAGES. IN ALMOST ten years of recovery and working with addicts attempting recovery, I saw very few couples keep their marriages intact. My marriage today is stronger than it has ever been. I attribute that most of all to the grace of God. I don't believe Ellyn and I could have stayed married without our belief in Him. However, the recovery of my marriage began with a wife who wouldn't give up and the treatment center's family therapy program.

People raised in a household that engenders shame tend to marry other shame-based people. Ellyn and I both brought our shame with us into the marriage. The result of the marriage of two shame-based people is a lack of real intimacy. It is difficult to be intimate when you feel like a defective person. This lack of intimacy is sustained by poor communication – fighting for control, giving in rather than negotiating, blaming, avoiding, and escaping. I escaped to work, anonymous sex, and pornography. Ellyn learned from her hypercritical father and insecure grandmother not to make waves, even when she disagreed. She gave in to avoid conflict and developed her own resentments. She had difficulty asking and receiving and escaped into depression. But she did not give up.

The first day of family therapy was honesty day. Healthy marriages are based on honesty; ours was not. I had lied about my behavior; we both lied to avoid conflict. I was instructed to bring a letter to Ellyn that was honest about my behavior. Ellyn was to tell me how my addiction hurt had her. Right up until that day, I had minimized everything I had told Ellyn about my addiction. That afternoon I told her the truth. Ellyn was hurt one more time. She felt depressed, angry, and afraid. She had been publicly humiliated when the police came to the house. Her father had abandoned her; now her husband had. How could I do this to her? How many lies can a marriage endure? At the end of the first day, I was not sure that Ellyn would return the next morning. I could not blame her if she chose not to come back.

The following morning, I stood anxiously on the hill overlooking the parking lot, wondering if my thirty-seven-year marriage had survived. When I saw Ellyn's car pull into the lot, I first felt relieved, then elated. My marriage had survived the results of my dysfunctional behavior for at least one more day.

The second day brought more stress and tension. Toni, the therapist, led us through a discussion of our family history. Addiction runs in families, and we could both see that there were examples in both our families. I had been in therapy for almost three months, while Ellyn had been home alone. Today she learned many of the things that I had learned over the past three months. She began to see that my addiction was more than just deficient morality, that it was a disease that came from my genetics and my background. The discussions were difficult for both of us. Afterwards Ellyn was so exhausted that the staff found a place for her to take a nap.

The family therapy portion of the program was over, but Toni realized that it was not enough. She could see the pain Ellyn was in, the loneliness and isolation she felt. I was still in treatment, receiving therapy; Ellyn was still alone at home. Toni was treating June, the wife of a former patient whose husband was now in prison. June was getting meaningful support from COSA (codependents of sex addicts), a recovery program not too far from our home. At Toni's encouragement, June invited Ellyn to join her at a meeting.

The meeting was a revelation for Ellyn. There were over forty wives and girlfriends of sex addicts present, suffering the same pain that Ellyn experienced. They were dealing with the pain by talking about it, helping each other, trying to learn how to recover from codependency. Ellyn was no longer alone. In those rooms, Ellyn would begin her own recovery.

Codependency

Through regular participation in recovery groups, Ellyn learned that she was codependent. Codependency involves dysfunctional thoughts, feelings, and behaviors, primarily learned in childhood, that sabotage relationships with self and others. A simple definition says that Ellyn was addicted to me, although it's not that simple. Ellyn depended on me for her happiness, her contentment, and in many ways her reason for being. I could not meet those needs. Ellyn believed that her love and her hard work raising our children were what were needed to meet my needs. They were not. I needed her to be the person who she is today: alive, spontaneous, caring for herself as well as for me.

The dysfunctions that helped us to survive childhood do not serve us well as adults. Ellyn's symptoms arose from her own childhood, from the trauma of her mother dying as a result of Ellyn's birth, from a bitter perfectionist father, and overprotection by the grandparents who raised her. As she immersed herself in the programs of recovery groups, she saw the opportunity to change herself and began to do so. I appreciate her help in writing this section.

Self-Esteem

Ellyn and I had been dancing the dysfunctional dance of codependence for thirty-seven years. Both of us suffered from low self-esteem, a negative self-evaluation. Ellyn lacked confidence in herself, was insecure and self-critical. Her esteem was based on what others thought of her. She was, and still is, a beautiful seamstress and tailor, but was never satisfied until others complimented her on her work. She was starved for the compliments she did not receive as a child, but when they came, she pushed them away. When good things happened to her she didn't think she was worthy of them. Ellyn lacked a healthy internal sense of self-worth.

My lack of self-esteem showed up as arrogance or grandiosity. I grew up with the unhealthy dichotomy of low self-esteem that came from the excessive criticism of my mother and the bullying of my peers, and an undeserved sense of self-confidence that I learned from being a high-IQ child. I could not admit

I was wrong, even when I knew I was. I trusted myself but could not trust others. I could not ask for help, even when I was in great despair.

We wish we could live a problem-free life, but life can be full of problems. For many of us, they seem to come at us endlessly, one after another. Children learn to make decisions and solve problems in their childhood family. When a child is raised in an overprotective home where decisions are made for them, she can later feel overwhelmed by the normal problems she would face as an adult. Ellyn was afraid to make decisions for fear they would be wrong and her father would punish her. Her aunt Elizabeth had become pregnant while in college, and her grandmother did not want that to happen to Ellyn. Ellyn was told to go to school and to come straight home. She was not allowed to participate in after-school activities nor have a normal social life. Because of overprotection, the conflict in her childhood home, and her low self-esteem, Ellyn learned to hate discord and to give in rather than attempt to resolve a problem. The problem remained, compounded by resentment.

As a child, I learned to solve problems, even thrive on them. As an adult, I spent much of my time at work resolving problems. I came home, ready to relax, to an accumulation of unsolved problems, often problems involving the children. Ellyn was ready for me to help her solve the problems. But rather than help her solve the problems, I would jump in and solve them my way. But solving them my way didn't resolve them to Ellyn's satisfaction. Her resentment grew, and her self-esteem fell even lower.

All human beings are imperfect people. When we see things as perfect or imperfect, as absolutely black or absolutely white, polar opposites with no middle ground, we deny the basic truth of human beings: we are all naturally imperfect. Any relationship in which we engage will inevitably be flawed. But having been raised in perfectionist homes, neither of Ellyn nor I would believe that it was okay to be imperfect, and we let our imperfections damage our own self-esteem.

Ellyn would take apart, many times, a gorgeous dress that she had created in order to eliminate an invisible flaw, trying to make it perfect. She was seldom satisfied with the beauty of her creations. I would correct the smallest errors of others, and also hers, not accepting imperfections. We wanted each other to be perfect, to have the perfection we demanded of ourselves. But we could not have perfection in ourselves or our partner. We grew disappointed and resentful.

Boundaries

The Serenity Prayer, often used in recovery groups, asks:

> God, grant me the serenity to accept the things I cannot change, courage to change the things I can, and wisdom to know the difference.[xx]

The prayer asks God to give us boundaries. When we have healthy boundaries, we take responsibility for ourselves, for our own thoughts and behaviors. These are things we can change. Good boundaries also tell us not to take responsibility for the thoughts and behaviors of others, things that are beyond our ability to change anyway. When our boundaries are broken or damaged, we have trouble separating our own thoughts and behaviors from those of our codependent. We allow ourselves to take advantage of others, or we allow ourselves to be abused.

Ellyn and I had boundary issues. She seemed to have an endless list of household projects she would drop on me and expect them to be done immediately, with no consideration for my plans and desires. They were things that needed to be done, often things that she expected me to see, but I did not. She would hold her desires in and then dump them on me all at once. I resented those demands. She saw me not as another person, but as an extension of her agenda for the family

At other times, Ellyn was unable to say "no." I was committed to my career and often put the needs of my job ahead of the needs of my family. My demands crossed her boundaries. I would ask her to go out to dinner with me and a business associate. She had other plans, but would say "yes" and then resent going. More dramatically, I would accept a new job requiring a cross-country move. Ellyn would prefer not to move but give in and say "yes," and then would harbor resentment.

Many of my boundaries had disappeared. I had lost my way into a false self-confidence and eventually into pornography and infidelity. Good boundaries tell us to be respectful of the rights of others. Spouses have the right to the time and attention of their partner. That boundary is violated when he spends hours on the computer. Children have the right not to be sexually abused and photographed. I did not respect their right not to have their photograph viewed and passed from computer to computer to fulfill the erotic desires of strangers. Boundaries tell us to take responsibility for our actions.

Perceptions of Reality

At times, both Ellyn and I struggled to understand or express who we really were. As she was growing up, Ellyn's grandparents would engage in loud arguments, shouting and screaming vile things at each other. When Ellyn would later ask her grandmother why she and her grandfather were fighting, her grandmother would deny the fight ever happened. Ellyn's great uncle committed suicide. Ellyn heard all the details at school from the other children: that he had hung himself and what he looked like. When Ellyn got home, however, her family denied everything. "What are you talking about? That didn't happen." These things left Ellyn feeling unsure of her own reality.

Ellyn would deny her feelings. I would call home and ask how she was. Ellyn would say, "I'm fine." But her voice said the reality was something entirely different. It said, "I smashed up the car" or "The children are out of control and you're not here to help." Frustrated, I would respond in a dysfunctional way by not calling again. After being raised in a home full of denial, it was easy for Ellyn to deny my addiction, even when there was enough evidence that she would have known.

I denied my own reality in different ways. I remember clearly the wife of a friend who said one day in conversation, "We're nice-looking people." My brain immediately thought, "No, I'm not." My brain unconsciously traveled back to the shame of the small, immature boy who wanted to look like the high school athletes. Today I still look much younger than my age. What was a disadvantage at age fourteen is an advantage in my sixties. Many of my peers would be delighted to look like I look now. I struggle to accept the truth of my own reality. Did my addiction to pornography relate back to my ancient and inaccurate view of my own body, the desire to be someone else? Was it the unrealistic negative view of my own body that pushed me toward the fantasy and unreality of pornography and anonymous sex and away from the reality of my own family? I don't know. However, I know that as a pornography addict, I knew what I was doing but did not admit it. Shame kept me from accepting my own reality.

Relationships
Neither of us accepted normal dependence on each other. Codependents don't ask for the things they need. Ellyn was a dependent person who expected other people to meet her needs and desires. She knew what she wanted and expected other people to know what she wanted too, as if we were mind readers. Ellyn would ask if I wanted to go to the movies with her, and I would decline because I had other plans or didn't like that movie. She would resent the refusal. Soon she would stop asking, assume I would say no, and resent the refusal that I didn't make. She assumed that she would never get what she wanted. Ellyn became afraid to make even the smallest decision without my agreement. "Should I spend $7 for that blouse that's on sale?" If Ellyn wanted a hug, she expected me to know and provide it, but would never ask for it. I wouldn't know, and she wouldn't tell me.

I had a different problem. I didn't always know what I needed or desired. When I did know, I didn't ask for help. I had learned in my own dysfunctional childhood that asking for help would be met with rejection, with bitterness and perfectionist demands. I had learned that if I had a problem it would be best to solve it myself. I did not share my feelings and did not ask for help, even if that meant that my own needs would not be met. I became anti-dependent, ignoring my own wants and needs but not satisfying hers either. I was self-centered and didn't think of Ellyn's needs. Ellyn would try hard to meet my needs, but didn't know what they were. She didn't ask, and I didn't tell her. I would not share the frustrations that I brought home from work, would not express my own emotions. I stopped sharing the thoughts and feelings that are necessary for an intimate relationship. I hid my feelings even from myself. I wouldn't ask, and would do without.

Two codependent individuals who grew up in a childhood of physical, emotional, or sexual abuse usually find it difficult to be intimate in an adult relationship. Intimate people are able to share themselves with their spouse and allow their spouse to share as well, without either attempting to change the other. For a couple to be intimate, they both must be able to identify their own needs and desires and know to ask the other to help them when they have a legitimate need they can't take care of by themselves. When one partner is too dependent and relies on the other to provide her needs and desires, intimacy is disrupted. The connection is more like a parent/child than a marriage. If one partner is anti-dependent and never asks for help, intimacy is disrupted because he does not share his needs and desires, so his partner cannot respond to them. For Ellyn and me, intimacy was a difficult struggle.

Empathy involves vicariously experiencing the thoughts, feelings, and experience of another person, feeling how others feel, sharing their happiness, experiencing their pain. Empathy is critical to intimacy. Codependents think they have empathy for each other, but they seldom do. I did not feel Ellyn's depression the way she felt it. She felt despair; I felt my own resentment. Ellyn did not feel the frustration I brought home from work. Until we understood our own feelings, we could not begin to understand the feelings of each other. Ellyn saw me through the impaired experiences of her childhood. I saw Ellyn through the fog of my dysfunctional youth.

Extremes

One way children learn to experience reality through extreme actions comes from being ignored as a child. If Ellyn talked to her grandmother while she was cleaning the house, her grandmother would continue cleaning and not even look at Ellyn. Ellyn felt she was not as important as grandmother's clean house, very close to the way I felt less important than my mother's living room rug. Children learn to act in an excessive manner to attract the attention they need. These behaviors, which are necessary for children, don't simply go away as we grow older.

Depression served this need for Ellyn as an adult. I quickly learned that was how Ellyn acted to gain my attention. I knew the depression was real, but I felt manipulated. I would discount her pain, or flee from it. Ellyn's realities tended to be black and white, all or nothing. We were unable to negotiate issues as critical as how to discipline our children because there was no middle ground. Ellyn over-disciplined. I under-disciplined. I stopped trying to find a middle ground because we never succeeded in finding one. We did not resolve the issues and both felt resentful.

Resentment occurs when we feel someone is taking advantage of us. Much of our resentment occurs when we try to control others. Ellyn thought it was my responsibility to take out the trash, an idea that came out of her childhood. She wanted it taken out in the morning when, she thought, the animals would not get into it. I wanted to take out the trash before I went to bed. I thought she not only wanted the trash taken out, she wanted to control how I did it. In the morning, my mind was focused on going to work, an idea that came out of my childhood. So I said, "Fine, I'll take the trash out if I can take it out at night. If you want it taken out in the morning, you'll have to do it. Ellyn took the trash out most weeks, but was resentful.

Ellyn wanted to punish me for not taking out the trash. I regularly purchased old baseball cards for my collection. They were shipped insured, and had to be picked up at the post office. I worked outside the home; Ellyn did not, so I expected her to pick them up, just as my mother would have. Ellyn resented that I would not take out the trash when she wanted it taken out, but expected her to pick up the baseball cards. I felt she didn't respect the importance of my job and the income I provided for the family. Ellyn picked up the cards, but the resentment was compounded. She sank into depression. The dance of codependence continued.

COMMITMENT

I have attempted to show you an illustration of the sources of codependence and addiction, how they emerged from the dysfunction of our childhood and how we experience them as adults. We had no control over our childhood experiences; they were not our fault. But they embedded themselves in our life as a disease, like diabetes, that will take more than willpower to control.

Hardships drive some people apart. Most marriages do not survive addiction, codependence, and long prison sentences. Others grow closer. Despite all the problems in our marriage, Ellyn and I had a friendship and trust forged by common values and experiences. Both of us recognized that change would be difficult. But if both partners are committed, most of their differences can be resolved.

By itself, insight does not change the behaviors we learned in childhood. But, as Ellyn and I learned more about the motivations that we brought with us from our childhood, we slowly learned how to change. To change, we needed help. We'll talk more about that in the pages ahead.

CHAPTER 19

Learning About Recovery

I LEARNED THAT MANY THINGS can influence the chance of an individual's recovery, including the age of onset of the illness; frequency and intensity of the compulsive behaviors; degree of their subjective distress and remorse; their intelligence, self-observing capacity, sense of humor, and sense of responsibility; their general capacity to form interpersonal connections; motivation for change; and the presence of family and social support; and employment stability.[xxi] Recovery is also impacted by the degree of underlying character pathology; the co-occurrence of other psychiatric disorders and addictions; and the ability to engage in treatment, including financial and other logistical considerations, as well as the ability to develop a therapeutic alliance with helping professionals and peers.[xxii]

Interventions are techniques the addict can use to stop the addictive cycle before acting out. Such interventions promote recovery.

To the addict, obsessions are intrusive thoughts and fantasies that enter the addicts mind without his control. Once the addict recognizes the desirability of decreasing or ceasing engagement with the addiction, he can plan to stop the behavior early in the cycle. Thought-stopping is a way to interrupt these upsetting and dangerous thoughts and images in an early stage of the addiction cycle, before the obsession or acting out take hold. One form of thought-stopping uses mild self-punishment to take the addict's mind away from the internal talk and fantasies. For example, the addict can put a large rubber band on his wrist. Each time an inappropriate sexual thought, fantasy, or urge to act out enters the addict's mind, he pulls the rubber band away from his wrist and snaps it hard enough to cause mild pain. This draws his attention away from his negative thoughts and behavior; he interrupts their flow.

Other methods can be used to interrupt the obsessions as they occur. One way is counting backward by 7's from a high number. The addict simply picks a starting number whenever the obsession enters her consciousness, a different number each time, and begins counting backwards: e.g., 395, 388, 381, 374, 367, 360. If the addict keeps counting, the obsession eventually disappears. When she counts long enough and often enough, she breaks the thought process. Addicts may design their own thought-stopping methods, like sighting the colors of the rainbow in the environment around them, breaking into prayer for the person fantasized in the obsession, or singing a hymn.

Other techniques can interrupt the obsession. If the obsession begins as a person is waking up in the morning, simply getting out of bed may interrupt the unwanted thoughts. If the obsession occurs during the day, the addict can phone a friend or visit a coworker in the next cubical. For others, exercise breaks the pattern. It is hard to think of anything else when playing table tennis or racquetball. The key for the addict is to plan to do whatever works to stop the obsession before it progresses further into the addiction cycle.

Psychologists use many other interventions to help reduce unwanted behaviors. Covert sensitization is a cognitive-behavioral intervention in which addicts are trained to remember the extremely negative consequences at the low point of their disease in order to override any positive associations. The consequences can be associated with the deviant behavior in an emotional and powerful way. For example, I can imagine myself looking at child pornography when a dozen armed police officers pound on my front door. I remember the fear and shame I felt when I realized my behavior was going to be exposed, my job and reputation destroyed. I have remembered the horrified look on my wife's face when she realized I had been looking at child pornography. When I can recall these events at times I am tempted to act out, the memories serve as powerful deterrents, reminding me of the negative consequences from my addiction, displacing the short-term rewards.

Sexual arousal can be measured by several different measuring devices. Some sex offenders are required to have their sexual arousal measured using a penile plethysmograph.[xxiii] Seated in a small closet and hooked to the device, the offender places a small piece of heavy foil or a small expandable cord around his penis to measure blood flow. He then views pictures of men and women, boys and girls of all ages, and at the same time listens to recorded stories of sexual seduction or sexual violence. Penile blood flow is measured to show what arouses him sexually.

In some cases, the offender is well aware of what sexually arouses him. In other cases, his knowledge of his own arousal patterns has become so distorted as a result of years of viewing pornography or objectifying others that he does know what arouses him. In some cases, he is so ashamed of his own arousal pattern that he lies about it. Some people are aroused by violence; other are not. Some are aroused by a very narrow age range of children; others have a broader range of arousal. Once the arousal patterns become clear, a protocol can be developed to address the particular triggers. Many experts believe that arousal patterns can be changed or aborted.

Some therapists attempt to change the arousal pattern from a deviant pattern to a healthy one; for example, a therapist may seek to transfer the arousal from children to adults, while other therapists seek to extinguish the arousal. Aversive therapy helps the addict reduce the unwanted behavior by helping him associate the behavior with negative physical stimuli. Seeking to change the arousal pattern from a deviant pattern to a healthy one, an addict can be instructed to begin a deviant obsession, and then be given an electrical shock when he becomes aroused. Some sex offenders may be given ammonia capsules and told to break one open under their nose and breathe in the pungent small whenever they have a deviant fantasy. If this is done consistently, the deviant thinking may be extinguished and the arousal pattern changed.

Aversive therapy is often used with orgasmic reconditioning. Tim, a voyeur, was told to masturbate thinking of his usual fantasies, but to substitute a healthy fantasy just before he ejaculated. As time passed he moved the healthy fantasies earlier in the masturbation process until eventually they replaced the deviant fantasy.

In therapy I met William, a pedophile who was attracted to very young girls. He was asked not to masturbate for a week. Then he was told to privately masturbate to healthy thoughts of an adult woman until a young girl entered his fantasies. When that happened, he was to stop. William had never had a healthy fantasy, so the therapy group had to help him develop one. He measured the length of time before a young girl entered his fantasy. This time became longer and longer until, eventually, he was able to ejaculate to a healthy fantasy of an adult woman. His arousal pattern was changing.

Anxiety and stress are drivers of the addiction cycle, and reducing stress helps the power of the addiction abate. Comprehensive stress reduction programs help people identify stressful events, monitor their stress, and act to reduce it. Addicts in recovery often find that journaling helps with this process, or keeping a daily record to better recognize and monitor the thoughts, feelings, and behaviors that signal the addictive process.

Various types of meditation and relaxation methods train the recovering addict to reduce stress and anxiety. Breathing exercises train the individual to consciously take a series of slow, rhythmic deep breaths that counteract the arousal of the sympathetic nervous system, the system that mediates our stress. Using progressive muscle relaxation, the individual may also reduce tension by consciously relaxing special muscle groups in sequence. In transcendental meditation, the meditator focuses on a mantra, repeating a name, syllable, or sound. In guided imagery, the meditator visualizes relaxing, calming images, perhaps a sunny beach, a quiet forest, or a field of grain gently blowing in the wind. The recovering individual may practice forming such images until they can be recalled easily whenever tension and anxiety begin to build.

Exercise can also reduce stress and anxiety. Full-body exercise, such as swimming, running, dancing, table tennis, and many other sports usually works best. Exercise increases circulation, improves muscle tone, and releases hormones. Dr. John Ratey, in his book *Spark,* explains that exercise is "activity dependent" and over time instills a sense of well-being. It also reduces the urge to act out by building detours around existing connections that previously have led automatically to addictive behavior.

Most sex addicts have spent a huge number of hours preparing for, engaging with, and recovering from their acting out behaviors: masturbating, cruising for prostitutes, seeking the right victim, searching for the right images on the computer, and coping with the shame afterwards. Once abstinent, unless they learn to fill their newly available time with constructive and gratifying activity, they are likely to slip back into addictive behavior. One reason twelve-step programs are effective in helping people stay sober is that the fellowship provides new activities and a large and diverse social network for those who are willing to participate. Those trying to stop their addictive behavior need to plan new and rewarding activities to replace their addiction.

In *A Group Therapists Guide to Process Addictions,* Korshak, Nickow, and Strauss explain that addiction is not an acute disease that can be quickly cured but rather, a chronic disease, which, with effective treatment, can become dormant[xxiv]. Research studies have now identified a natural recovery process for some addictions; for example, one-third of pathological gamblers are thought to lead a normal life, free of their addictive behaviors, without professional treatment or self-help programs.[xxv] Unfortunately, many individuals remain vulnerable, experiencing cravings to re-engage in addictive behavior, sometimes for many years and even for life, even after stable recovery has been achieved. Furthermore, twelve-step participants note that an addict may be "dry" but not sober; that is, abstinent for many years without being involved in a recovery process. Personality distortions resulting from the addictive process often persist, even when the individual is able to abstain from active addictive behavior. On the other hand, an individual may be actively in his addiction and, by working a treatment program, experience many of the benefits of recovery.

Because the consequences may be grave should they relapse, many recovering addicts continue to work a program that fosters abstinence and furthers recovery for many years or even for life. For example, an individual may continue to regularly attend twelve-step meetings, socialize with others in the recovery community, and pray or meditate on a regular basis. He or she also may choose to stay in a recovery group for many years or even decades to monitor his or her addiction, maintain abstinence, and enhance his or her recovery. Many individuals who achieve recovery become conscientious and deliberate about maintaining their place in their family and social community, an active involvement in creative projects, and their ethical and spiritual values; these may become part of their lifestyle. These practices not only create a buffer against returning to addictive behaviors, but also become gratifying in their own right.

Twelve-step participants speak of humility, acceptance, and gratitude as attitudes that protect a recovering individual from relapse. Those who achieve recovery may experience the satisfaction sought, but not achieved, from the addictive process – possibly greater gratification from life than the average person experiences. According to Roshi Phillip Kapleau "Dryness, rigidity and self-centeredness give way to a flowing warmth, resiliency and compassion, while self-indulgence and fear are transmuted into self-mastery and courage."[xxvi] Recovery, beyond mere abstinence from the addiction processes, can *initially* create a sense of well-being, trust, and hope, and *ultimately* a transcendent experience of daily life, filled with wonder and awe.[xxvii]

I began writing this book from a sincere belief that in my case and in the case of others I have known, participation in twelve-step programs and professional treatment supporting the twelve steps can effectively secure recovery. I do not know if this is true for everybody, but it is true for me.

I absorbed the education about addiction that my counselors gave me when I was in treatment. They started my learning about the biology and neurology of addictions, some of which I am presenting here. Knowing about my powerlessness over these factors shifted me from shame to curiosity. I wanted to know more.

In twelve-step meetings I learned that my story is not unique; rather, it is typical for those afflicted with this illness. I heard my story in the stories of others. I was able to develop objectivity about the disease when I would hear someone else talking about their struggles. Listening to others, I learned their tools, tricks, and techniques to avoid the cycle of addiction; I also developed some of my own. The twelve steps became a guide for living my life free from addictive behavior. I saw the freedom and serenity available for others when they achieved abstinence and sobriety, and I did what they did because I wanted what they had. The addiction became smaller and smaller in my own psychological world, and my acting out behavior lessened and then ceased.

CHAPTER 20

Humility

Even while undergoing intensive treatment, I knew that relapse remained a possibility because the obsessions were still there. They continued to return particularly at bedtime and in the early morning. Of concern to me, they were sometimes enjoyable. The addictive cycle was embedded in my brain, waiting. I was one slip, one poor decision away from relapsing into addictive behavior all over again. Addiction is a sneaky and progressive disease; twelve-step programs call it "cunning, baffling, and powerful." The fear of my addiction returning was always with me.

To stop the addiction cycle and to stay stopped, I had to admit that relapse remained a constant possibility and recognize that simply stopping the behavior for a while was not a permanent solution. When I had been in treatment for about two months and had not looked at pornography or acted out sexually in any way for six months, I remained nervous about my ability to abstain from relapsing and falling back into my former secret, unmanageable life.

Triggers are cues that tell an addict's brain to go on automatic, to reenter the addiction cycle. Triggers can be almost anything – a quick scene on television, a fragrant bar of soap, a stressful moment, a euphoric memory, or a particular person. They hijack the brain's neurocircuitry and quickly move the addict into the addiction cycle. Some therapists recommend that addicts leaving treatment centers change the familiar associations – places, people, and things – that can trigger the cycle. Addicts in recovery sometimes say: "Stop acting out, and change your whole life."

Relapse prevention prepares the addict for troubling situations. I talked with my therapist, Anne. She put it bluntly: "Brady, you couldn't stop before because you didn't know how. Now you do." And when I stopped I hadn't known how to stay stopped. Now I did. I needed to establish boundaries regarding computer use, traveling alone, movies I should not see, and books that I could not safely read. Any of these things could trigger my addiction cycle. I no longer use the Internet. I do not travel alone. I do watch movies or read books with sexual content. I have a long list of friends to call when I feel myself isolating. Every addict has different triggers and needs to establish his own boundaries and diversions around the people, places, and things that can trigger the old behavior and begin the cycle again.

Some changes can be even more difficult, like leaving a relationship or quitting a job. I was told that nothing in my life was more important than abstinence from my addictive behaviors. Some addicts have asserted, "If you don't put your recovery first, you will lose whatever else you put ahead of your recovery, as you roll back downhill toward the gutter." If a relationship is triggering an addiction, the relationship needs to be repaired or ended. If a job is triggering an addiction, the job needs to be changed or terminated. At some point, the addict needs to become willing to go to any length and do whatever it takes to establish and maintain abstinence.

To avoid triggers, it is important that the recovering sex addict takes care with seemingly unimportant decisions. Several of those decisions in my life prior to my arrest had led me into addiction. In treatment I became extremely aware that little decisions can have major consequences. I was driven once a week to sessions at an offsite location. The direct route along the interstate highway passed a XXX video store, a trigger for me. I did not want to trigger my addiction cycle. Before we arrived at the point where I could see the store, I trained myself to focus my eyes in the other direction. I asked the driver to tell me when we had passed the video store so I could look straight ahead again. Even today I will drive miles out of my way to avoid driving past a XXX video store.

Karl was a recovering addict I met in my twelve-step group. He told the story of driving to an evening Bible study session at his church. Because he was a little late, he cut through a neighborhood he usually avoided. A prostitute he used to visit was standing on a corner. His addiction cycle was triggered. A seemingly unimportant decision, a shortcut through an old neighborhood, pulled Karl back into his addictive behavior. He did not make it to church that evening. After three days of acting-out behavior, he came back to our meetings. Some recovering members, once in a relapse, do not ever come back.

In the treatment center I was required to complete a "thoughts and feelings journal" every day. I was to identify three things that happened during the day, what I thought about them, and how I felt. Months later, when I looked back on my work, I recognized how much these writings evidenced my recovery. In my addiction, only lust was meaningful to me; everything else seemed like a distraction. Over time, however, in treatment, my thoughts and feelings about nonsexual activities moved from negative to positive. As I stopped focusing with the lens of my addiction, I became gradually able to see positive things that occurred during the day. I began to positively experience events that I would have previously seen negatively, as impediments. For example, I began to notice the beauty of the pink sky just before sunrise. When a program friend was annoyed with his girlfriend's ways, I saw an opportunity to demonstrate compassion. When a staff member complained about my leaving my socks on the floor, I saw an opportunity for me to change my patterns.

I knew that I had little time to spend with my family between the time I left treatment and the time I would report to prison for a lengthy, although still undetermined, time. Ellyn visited me every weekend. We sat on the deck overlooking gentle hills and beautiful trees, and talked. One afternoon we watched a strange and interesting roadrunner run across the field, roll on the dusty walking trail, and jump up the side of a tree to his nest, looking like a puffball with the dust bouncing like smoke off his feathers into the air. Despite the tension caused by my deviant behavior and our unknown future, Ellyn's visits were a relaxing time. I grew anxious to go home.

The staff had other ideas. I was committed to remaining at the treatment center until the staff agreed I was well into recovery and ready to leave, and after three months at the treatment center it was suggested that I spend some time volunteering in the community while continuing to live at the treatment center. Sex addiction is a disease of self-centeredness and selfishness; it was important that I spent time being of service to others. Not many places are anxious to accept a convicted sex offender as a volunteer, but I discovered a food and clothing bank sponsored by a local church. They needed a truck driver and general warehouse hand, and they were glad to have my help. This ministry served the very poor – unemployed, migrant, and homeless, families displaced by fires or other disasters. They charged nothing for food or clothing. I learned that no matter how bad off I was, there were others in even worse shape. I found myself not only driving the truck, but donating the gas as well.

I spent my evenings attending recovery meetings. I was surprised to find there were nightly meetings of recovering sex addicts in several nearby communities. I attended a twelve-step meeting for recovery from sex addiction every day for seven months. Multiple programs exist; although they vary slightly, they share a common purpose of helping the addict recover. I found a "sponsor," Roy, a mentor who had been in sober recovery from sex addiction for thirteen years. He met with me regularly, answered questions, and led me into the path of recovery that has guided me ever since.

After four and a half months I was discharged from the treatment center, having successfully completed their program, and moved back home. Fear of the unknown had become a constant feature of my life. I needed to stay busy and keep my mind on activities that were healthy for me. I said the Serenity Prayer many times a day.

There were many things I could not change – my past behavior, the reactions of other people, and the length of my sentence – but I was never helpless. I could, with help, change my own attitude and current behavior. I always had an array of steps I could take to further my recovery. I continued helping at the food bank twice each week, played golf with Bruce at least once a week, and went to my recovery meetings every night.

Ellyn wanted to move to a smaller house and a new neighborhood. So much of her life had revolved around my career. I would be gone; Ellyn wanted to start over too. We purchased a lot in a new community where most of our neighbors were retired. Ellyn and I designed our new home, not knowing if I would ever live there. While I was in prison, Ellyn would sell the old house and oversee construction of the new one. We began to build a new, still uncertain future, terrified that a very long sentence would cause there to be no future at all.

CHAPTER 21

Sentencing

MY SENTENCING WAS SCHEDULED FOR Tuesday, April 27, 2005, in federal court. It was my youngest son Larry's twenty-second birthday. My older sons, Brady and Fred, flew in to also be present. Our family met Monday in Wayne's office to review strategy for the sentencing hearing. Brady was to represent the family, and a psychiatrist would report about my time in treatment. I began to outline a statement admitting my guilt and expressing regret.

Ninety-five percent of those charged with federal crimes plead guilty. Most are offered a plea agreement that recommends sentencing at the lower end of the sentencing guidelines in return for their guilty plea. The low end of the guidelines for my crime of receipt and distribution of child pornography would be 17 ½ years. I was not offered a plea agreement. Mine was a public case, and any leniency could bring public criticism. Months earlier the prosecutor had agreed that if I cooperated and if no evidence of other crimes turned up, he would consider not recommending a specific sentence to the judge. That would give the judge the leeway to sentence me below the guidelines if he chose to do so. That left the judge, who had a lifetime appointment, to be the potential recipient of public anger. The prosecutor made no guarantees, and we had no idea what the judge would do. I could go to prison for the rest of my life.

Filled with apprehension, my family and I left Wayne's office shortly before 9 a.m. Tuesday morning and walked the long block to the courthouse. This time there were no television cameras waiting there. An early morning murder had drawn them away. Seated in the courtroom with my family were a handful of friends. Roy, my twelve-step sponsor, was there, along with several employees from the treatment center. My golfing friend Bruce was there, as were some friends from church and some friends of Ellyn. I appreciated their support. Also present were two reporters from the print media.

The judge arrived, and we made our presentations. The psychiatrist gave a detailed and inspiring report about my progress at the treatment center and his positive prognosis about my future behavior. Brady Jr. made a short but moving statement for my family. I gave a seven- minute statement admitting my guilt and expressing regret. Wayne attested that I was regretful and was serious about changing my life; he noted that since my arrest I had done everything I could to get help. The prosecutor did what he promised. He reminded the judge that the seriousness of my offense required a lengthy prison sentence, told him of my cooperation, and did not make a specific sentence recommendation.

The judge recessed the court, and we anxiously waited for his decision. Fear and trepidation accompanied me as I went back to the viewing gallery and thanked each of my friends for being present. As the recess extended to thirty minutes, a slight hopefulness intruded into the gloom that had penetrated my mind. Perhaps our presentation had made a difference. Perhaps the judge had heard what was said. We returned to our places as the judge reentered the courtroom. I felt paralyzed, going through trancelike motions similar to the ritual of my addiction cycle.

The judge reminded me that I had broken the law and broken trust with the community. He then stated: "Mr. C., I don't want you to die in prison, but you might. I sentence you to ninety-seven months in federal prison, and five years of supervised release." In the back of the courtroom, I heard my wife Ellyn scream. The judge went on to describe the conditions of my release, but I no longer heard anything. Over eight years! I had been terrified of a twenty-year sentence, but had hoped for much less. It would be months later, after I met others convicted of the same crime, that I realized how very fortunate I was. I was released on my own recognizance and told to report to prison in five weeks.

The tension lifted, since I now knew the answers to questions that had been tearing at me for over a year. Still inside me was the fear of prison, of the unknown. What would happen to a sixty-year-old sex offender in prison with drug dealers and thugs? My thinking quickly turned negative.

Our children circled around Ellyn. We worked together as a family, dividing our tax calculations, financial spreadsheets, and other major household projects among us. I attempted to throw away a lifetime accumulation of unneeded stuff. In five weeks I disposed of sixty-one years of memories that I would not need for the next eight years. I continued to attend recovery meetings every day. It was better to stay busy than to think about the unknown and forbidding future that lay ahead, and I believed I needed as many meetings as I could attend to achieve recovery from my disease.

CHAPTER 22

Prison

BEFORE MY ARREST I HAD not spent one minute considering the plight of people in prison. Now I was going to be one of them. One Tuesday morning in early June, I prepared to report to a federal correctional institution that was a one-hour drive from my home. Ellyn, Bruce, and I drove to the prison, where I would turn myself in. I had asked Bruce to drive because I did not want Ellyn to be alone. We arrived at the prison exactly on time. I stared at the twelve-foot walls with rolls of razor wire at the top and bottom, the armed guards in cars circling the fence.

Ellyn and I went inside, full of dread. We hugged and kissed, the emotion too difficult to describe. I took off my wedding ring and gave it to Ellyn, who was going to wear it on a necklace until I got home. The officer told me I could keep it, the one thing I could bring into the prison. I put the ring back on my finger, and then Ellyn left. I was escorted into the prison, alone and afraid.

I was taken to the receiving area and given a brief physical exam. Next, the staff warned me that sex offenses were considered the worst possible crimes by other inmates and instructed that I should lie about my offense and develop a story, a legend, to support the lie. I was already afraid; now my fear approached unmitigated terror. My civilian clothes were taken from me, and I put on the khaki uniform of a low-security federal prisoner that I would wear for the duration of my sentence. Still in shock, I was escorted to my housing unit.

Seven by ten feet, my new home contained two single cots, two small lockers for all our possessions, and two plastic chairs. The room had no door, no bars, and a secure window looking directly out at the fence topped by concertina wire. My new roommate was a middle-aged Columbian drug dealer who spoke very little English. He asked why I was in prison. I lied and told him "fraud."

I went from my room to the television room. A large, muscular, tattooed white man with a shaved head looked up and said, "Hey, here's a guy we saw on television!" My fable had lasted fifteen minutes. I was stuck. My attempt to hide the truth of my previous behavior had failed. Anxiety and desperation filled my mind and body, but I could do nothing. I would be living in a building with three hundred dangerous felons who were convinced I was a child molester, in a room with no door.

The consequences were swift. As I walked to the dining hall, other inmates began shouting at me "Chomo," which stood for child molester. Newspaper and magazine articles about me appeared on the bulletin boards. A copied announcement was posted in dozens of locations throughout the prison, inviting people to my room for sexual activity. I took the signs down when I saw them and did my best to ignore the harassment, but I was definitely afraid.

At 5:30 one morning, I was awakened by a corrections officer and told to go to the lieutenant's office. He had to point the way. Tall and thick-chested, the lieutenant's body reeked of intimidation. His first question was, "Why did you put up those signs?" Astonished at the accusation, I told him the truth. He asked if I was afraid. I lied. I knew the consequences of an honest answer would mean a move to protective custody – solitary confinement and loss of privileges—for my own safety, and a probable transfer to a new institution, further from friends and family. He assured me that those who put up the announcements would be caught and punished, but to my knowledge they were not.

There were some gifts. Mr. Hernandez, an Hispanic-American a few years older than I, lived across the hall. While visiting family in Mexico, he had been tempted by an offer of $5,000 to bring drugs across the border into the United States. "I decided to go for it," he told me. He was caught and was completing a five-year sentence. He told me if I wanted my marriage to survive prison, I should phone my wife every night. We were allowed three hundred telephone minutes per month, an average of ten minutes each day. When I had been traveling on business I often didn't call my wife for days on end. Selfishly, I thought, "She has my cell number; she can call me." In prison I began to call Ellyn every evening.

The small prison library was down the hall from my room. I went there most days to read the newspaper. One day my roommate came running into the library, nervous and jumpy. Someone had thrown coffee on my bed. He was afraid he would be punished because the room wasn't neat. By the time I got back to the room, Mr. Hernandez had already started the washing machine where I could put my bedding, a friendly gesture extended to me in a time of need.

Another day, some of my clothing, my radio, my watch, and other possessions that I had purchased at the prison commissary were stolen. It was the third time this had happened in two weeks. Mr. Penny, a tiny white man who lived nearby, brought me a pair of shower shoes. Other inmates chipped in to help me out. I learned there is a surprising amount of generosity in prison, and an intense dislike for thieves.

In the early mornings, I enjoyed walking on the circular path around a small park in the middle of the prison. Gene, another inmate, also walked there during the mornings; soon we were walking together. Gene had lived his entire life in a small, rural community. The family farm was losing money and had to be sold to pay debts. Gene had managed a small motel. When that closed he worked as a security guard. Life had not treated him well. Gene had chatted with a fifteen-year-old girl from Chicago on the internet. The girl shared stories about her hard life, living in poverty and frequently beaten by her abusive, alcoholic father. They also talked about sex. Foolishly, Gene sent her a bus ticket to his hometown in Nebraska. The fifteen-year-old girl turned out to be an FBI agent. Gene was sentenced to 9 ½ years in federal prison for soliciting a minor. Gene's roommate was leaving, and he asked me to be his new roommate. It turned out most of my problems had come from a next-door neighbor. The theft and harassment stopped when I changed rooms.

Every inmate had a job, with starting pay of 12 cents per hour and not going up much from there. Electricians and plumbers, clerks and tutors, librarians and janitors, cooks and dishwashers, all are inmates. My counselor, a large black man who looked like a preacher, assigned me as an orderly, a janitor in the housing unit where I lived. I began by cleaning walls, progressed through various janitorial functions, and eventually was assigned to a regular job cleaning bathrooms. The job was easy, and I was left with plenty of time to do the things I wanted to do. I never sought another job. I had gone from top corporate management to cleaning bathrooms, and didn't mind.

Prison has its own routine, and I learned to fit in. Our unit had three hundred inmates housed mostly in two-man rooms. We had central bathrooms, laundry rooms with washing machines and driers, and two large television rooms. There were a limited number of microwaves for heating food purchased at the commissary, and drinking fountains with hot water dispensers to make instant coffee. The comforts were limited. This was not Club Fed.

Despite the challenges I faced when I first arrived, I learned the prison was a reasonably safe place. Violent criminals were sent to higher-security prisons and only reached our facility after years of good conduct and nonviolent behavior. Most of the inmates were former drug dealers, many of them addicts dealing small amounts of drugs to support their addiction, or tempted by the incredible profits, far above what they could make otherwise. Sex offenders convicted of computer crimes were the second largest group. There were quite a few bank robbers, mostly men moved to robbery by the desperation of poverty and poor decision-making. Our low-security prison was considered a safe place for prominent individuals – former governors, prosecutors, police officers – and each of these were represented there.

The judicial system was created by our culture to deal with deviant behavior. Most inmates are selfish, immature, and have completely messed up their lives, trapped in the permanent adolescence of sports, gangs, risk, and fantasy. Many had nothing to start with and went downhill from there. They had limited social skills, anger management issues, and lack of appropriate moral reflexes. Almost half did not have a high school diploma or GED. In my case, I went to prison having destroyed a reputation I had spent a lifetime building.

Prison can be a barren, stark place, with too many people stored in very tight quarters. Some of the inmates are sociopaths, career criminals. We think that people are locked in prison for committing crimes, but that may be secondary to the more important issue of providing a home for defective and unfortunate people who were never properly prepared to manage on the outside. That partially explains why some keep returning to prison. Other otherwise ordinary folks sometimes make bad decisions – the first look at pornography, losing the rent money at a poker table, trying cocaine just once, that first drink of alcohol – that can poison their life and ultimately send them into a world where they never imagined they would be: federal prison.

As a man who had lived in a primarily white, educated society of people who worked hard, paid their bills, married, had children, coached Little League teams or served as Sunday school teachers, and lived what I saw as a "normal" life, it was a shock to find myself a minority in almost every way. I had spent most of my life with people who were educated and comparatively affluent. Until my arrest I had never known anyone who had been in prison. I was a racial minority in a prison of almost 50% Hispanic and 30% African-American men. A college graduate, I was also a minority in a prison population with little formal education. A sex offender, I was incarcerated in a population that harbored extreme anger at offenses against children, and hatred of those who committed them. Living and becoming friends with people whose backgrounds were so different from mine, often men in the depths of poverty, opened my eyes to a world I had never known.

CHAPTER 23

Separation

THE PRIMARY PUNISHMENT OF PRISON is separation – separation from people, from habits, from food, from life as I knew it. The most severe victim of my addiction and punishment was my family. All the things I had done to help Ellyn, she now had to do for herself. Ellyn had never dealt with a balky computer, made airplane reservations, negotiated with insurance companies, or managed our finances. Our children helped her, but the pressure fell on her shoulders. Ellyn had surgery to insert a stent in her artery. I could not be there to hold her hand or calm her fears. I was unable to be a real dad to our adult children. Larry got married. I could not be at his wedding, as the father I should have been. Our grandchildren were missing a grandfather. How could I ever correct the harm I had done to Ellyn, my sons, and my grandchildren? My love of camping and nature had prepared me to sleep on uncomfortable beds and eat crummy food. Nothing had prepared me or my family for the separation.

The key traits of addiction – dishonesty, self-centeredness, unmanageability – also destroy intimacy and relationships. The sex addict hungers for intimacy, yet spends an inordinate amount of time in sexual fantasy that interferes with his ability to be intimate with himself or others. His addictive actions lead to sex with no intimacy at all. The addict builds walls of shame, desolation, guilt, and loneliness that eventually isolate him from those who care about him. Sex can and should be inextricably tied to love, but the addict is so aroused by illicit relationships, whether directly or through pornography, that he fails to develop any truly intimate relationships.

Only after the addict admits the truth of his addiction and begins to overcome his self-hatred is he able to develop an intimate relationship with someone else. I learned that to help myself I had to look away from myself and toward my partner. Ellyn and I were faced with rebuilding the intimacy of our relationship while separated by a wall of steel. We were committed to doing so.

Although our separation was uncomfortable for both of us, in many ways it helped us. Ellyn learned to handle many of the things that I had taken care of when I was at home. Some examples are the challenges she faced when she sold our home and moved. Our home sold quickly, before our new home was built. Ellyn hired a transfer company to move, store, and deliver our household goods. Some of our possessions were damaged during the move, and others were missing. I would have dealt with those problems before, but this time Ellyn had to manage things herself. She went to the warehouse and found our lost antique chair in the warehouse office. An employee was sitting on it. A lost container of paintings and prints was being used as a trash container. Her success in completing the insurance claim and finding these previously lost possessions helped her self-confidence blossom like never before. She was becoming a self-sufficient person.

Her respect for the things I had quietly taken care of for thirty-seven years deepened. Ellyn learned to handle home repairs. She fought with the bank or credit card companies when our accounts were not accurate. Ellyn had traveled widely, but now she had to plan the trip and make the reservations. Each task was a challenge, a difficult step into areas I had taken care of before. Her respect for me and my role in the marriage increased, and her respect for herself grew even more as she succeeded in each new task. My respect for her grew too.

Ellyn and I spoke on the telephone every night. We compressed our days into ten-minute conversations. She visited me once a week and was able to experience some of the annoyances that I experienced as an inmate. Rules seemed to change every quarter, when the staff switched to new assignments. A tan skirt that Ellyn had worn several times was suddenly unacceptable when a new staff member decided it was khaki and not allowed. Ellyn returned home without visiting, angry that she had been treated like an inmate. Standards were inconsistent. Evening visits were supposed to begin at five o'clock, but seldom started before six. The waiting area was outside, where there were no toilet facilities and only an open shelter. Many visitors were elderly parents of inmates or wives visiting with young children. At times the wait to get in was as long as three hours. Corrections experts know that inmates with strong family support are less likely to reoffend, but families are often treated with no respect and become discouraged. Ellyn persisted.

The staff reminded us that there was "no sex in the living room." We were allowed a brief hug and kiss at the beginning of the visit and the end. Our only other physical contact was holding hands. Ellyn and I decided to spend our time in the visiting room working on improving our relationship. Sitting next to each other in a crowded room, we read the Bible together. We read books on apologizing, on forgiveness, and on strengthening our marriage. We read each chapter in advance of the visit in order to discuss it during our time together. We had long discussions about our childhoods, disclosing things that we had never revealed before. Slowly we developed a deeper understanding of how we had become the people we were. When the visit ended, I was strip-searched and returned to my housing unit. Ellyn drove home by herself.

What is unique in the relationship Ellyn and I have with each other is not that there are problems; every marriage has problems. What is special about our marriage is that it survived. Many people have asked Ellyn why she stayed with me. Very few marriages survive long prison sentences; ours has. Not many marriages survive sex addiction. We are not only still together; our marriage is growing and stronger than it ever was before.

We refer to each other as recovering; Ellyn is a recovering codependent, I am a recovering sex addict. I have no expectation that we will ever refer to ourselves as recovered. Likewise, I refer to our relationship as growing, as an ever-improving connection and kinship with no expectation of end or completion. We have changed the destructive cycle of addiction and codependence into a cycle of positive mental and sexual health, joy and happiness for both of us. Separation and prison played an important role in saving and strengthening our marriage.

CHAPTER 24

Finally Someone to Talk to Inside

THE FACT THAT MY CRIME had become public knowledge was beginning to become an advantage. It did not take long before other sex offenders began introducing themselves to me. Young and old, a commercial fisherman, a computer geek, a real estate attorney, a salesman, a corporate executive, and others were also in prison for possessing underage pornography. I learned there were hundreds of sex offenders in this prison, all told to lie about their offense. Finally, they heard of someone they could talk to openly and honestly, and they did.

Even federal criminal law recognizes that imprisonment is not an appropriate way of promoting correction. It simply takes people who don't follow society's rules off the street. As the original trauma of my arrival in prison and the harassment that followed it declined, I knew I needed to find my own way of rehabilitating myself. Lost in a world that was foreign to me, I knew it was best to spend my time with others who wanted to change their lives, and in the places where they gathered. I began to spend time in the library, the chapel, the education department, and at twelve-step meetings.

Prior to sentencing, I had taken my childhood friend Dr. Joe's advice and undergone an examination of my brainwaves, as well as neurological testing, which found no abnormalities. The last part of the neurological testing was an IQ test. The last question on the IQ test was, "Who wrote *Faust*?" I answered, "Goethe wrote *Faust*." The doctor asked if I had read it. I had not. There on the shelves of our small prison library was a copy of *Faust*, a story written in the 1600s of a man who sold his soul to the devil. Hadn't I done the same thing? Now I read *Faust*. During my time in prison I read about seven hundred books, from novels to spiritual essays to neuroscience, hoping to find ways to help me change into the person I wanted to become. The library became a safe place, a second home.

The education department offered classes taught by inmates. Those without a high school diploma were required to attend GED classes. For the rest of us there were inmate-led classes in languages, business and finance, parenting, computer use, and other skills. I studied Spanish, entrepreneurship, improved my keyboarding skills from 18 words per minute to 54, and completed a course in Microsoft Office and a community college course in Building Service Maintenance from the janitorial department. I also took psychology courses through distance learning programs from state universities to try to better understand my own inexplicable behavior. Education helped in my rehabilitation.

I began going to church every Sunday and attending Bible study on Thursday nights. It's natural for distressed men to seek comfort and guidance from a Higher Power; desperate people turn to religion when they have no place else to go. Many of those active in the prison's religious programs were sex offenders. I read the Bible regularly, paying more attention to the messages I had missed in my prior Christian life. In prison I found help and guidance from God that I had not found before and a freedom I had not known as an addict. I learned to pray in a different, more personal, way than I had prayed before. I developed a prayer expressing humility and gratitude:

> God, I've had so much success doing things my way, that when I came upon something I couldn't handle, and couldn't control, I didn't know what to do. I didn't have the power to stop. I had to find a power greater than I was – You. Thank you, God, for all the blessings you have given to me. Amen.

Our prison had twelve-step recovery programs for alcoholics and drug addicts. Although I was neither, I began attending these meetings. The programs focused on the fact that I was powerless and could not recover alone, and that

I needed to find a power greater than myself. I developed my relationship with God. I also developed relationships with others who, I believe, channeled the messages of God. The steps were the same as those in the twelve-step meetings for sex addicts I had attended before I went to prison, and I could relate to others in recovery. Often the stories these men told fit me as well; I resonated with the powerlessness, selfishness, and obsessions creating the addictive behavior, and for the need for a Higher Power to restore us to sanity. Each of the twelve-step programs was led by volunteers from outside the prison.

One evening Lee, a successful business owner, spoke of the final episode that brought him into recovery programs. He had been drinking all night and blacked out, unable to remember where he had been and what he had done. As his mind began to clear and he regained consciousness, he was standing on the side of a small rural road, attempting have sex with a fence post. I immediately thought, "I've never done *that*." But as I began to reflect on Lee's story I realized that I had been doing the same thing: engaging in sexual activity with people I did not know or care about. They might as well have been fence posts, as I treated them that way. The reality of my behavior was becoming more and more clear.

I had been in prison for over a year, and I missed having a group where I could talk honestly about sex addiction, like I'd had in the recovery groups I attended before I came to prison. An inmate friend, Jim, had been a minister in Iowa for thirty-one years before he succumbed to the temptations of child pornography. A learned, educated man fighting the enticement life had brought him, he had participated in twelve-step recovery programs for three years prior to his incarceration. He claimed that the twelve steps were America's greatest contribution to Christianity, as they brought lost people to God. I realized that was what I needed. When the prison chaplain invited a Christian organization to bring in a program that combined the twelve steps with support from the Bible, a program for recovery from all addictions, my roommate Gene and I decided to attend.

The small room was crowded. Our leader was a retired preacher who ran a transitional housing program for men coming out of prison. A short man with a trimmed white beard, he seemed surprisingly uncomfortable leading prison inmates. One of the inmates began a diatribe about sex offenders, and how they could not possibly be Christians. Our leader, the retired preacher, responded that while he didn't agree with everything the inmate said, sex offenders never stop offending. He would never allow one to live in his transitional housing. Stunned that an inmate could show such hatred in the chapel, and that a minister could support him, Gene and I walked out. This Christian program for "all" addictions didn't include ours.

The next day Gene and I talked to the chaplain, a direct man who we knew cared about us. He was shocked when he heard our story and assured us that he would speak with the program leader. He encouraged us to continue in the program, but it was too late. We could not rejoin a program led by a man who had written us off, a program with inmates who judged us and hated us for an offense they did not understand, who believed our sins were worse than theirs. We hated our own offense, but we had not given up on ourselves. We knew we could change our behavior. We would have to get help elsewhere.

Not only were there no programs for sex offenders in this prison, but even the prison psychologists were told they could not talk with us about sex. Gene and I asked the chaplain if he could arrange for a program intended just for us. Others had asked too. He agreed he would try, but it would be very difficult. The Bureau of Prison's policy was that all activities in the chapel were for all inmates. Most sex offenders in the prison were trying to keep their crime secret. They were afraid to come to a meeting where their very attendance would identify them as a sex offender, where any inmate, including those who hated us, could attend. But the chaplain was serious, and he searched for ways to get approval, and to find an outside organization to lead the program. A year later he received approval from the warden, but still had not found a sponsoring organization.

Gabe, an inmate, a sex offender from New York, was an active Messianic Jew, a Christian who also followed Jewish traditions. Gabe participated in many of the chapel programs. One evening he asked Wally, a volunteer from the community who taught Bible study in the prison, if he could stay an extra hour and lead a program for sex offenders. Wally was not a sex offender and knew nothing about addiction, but he loved the Lord, and his Christian faith drove his life. He was stunned by the idea. How could he lead a program for sex offenders? He told Gabe he would think about it.

Wally later recounted that as he left the room and walked down the hall, God spoke to him. "I love them, too," God said. Wally was not used to God speaking so clearly and directly. "I love them, too," echoed in his head. There was no question in Wally's mind that he had received an instruction from God. He walked directly to the chaplain's office and began planning a Christian study group for sex offenders.

God had talked to Wally, but the miracle was just beginning. The group began with eighteen inmates, invited by the chaplain or each other. Most were single or divorced, first-time offenders, men as lost as I was, whose life would never be the same as it had been. There was a carpenter, a boat captain, three young guys who had worked in the fast food industry, an unemployed motorcycle rider, a laborer, a retired soldier, a couple of computer technicians, a farmer, an EMT, a guy with one leg, and others I can't remember. They were a composite of men who struggled with sex addiction in the world outside. All were convicted sex offenders.

Here are stories of two of the men in our group:

Blake was a successful fifty-year-old engineer, married with children. He shared that he had struggled with a fetish since he was an early teen. His fetish desires led to masturbation, which became a daily habit. His fetish revolved around diapers. Until the internet, he thought he was the only one. The internet allowed him to connect with others, which was a great feeling of relief. He developed a desire to wear diapers at times, and to read stories about older kids who wore diapers. He found and collected online images of adults and children wearing diapers. He was arrested by the FBI. Ninety percent of the images he collected were legal, but they found some pictures of naked children being diapered. He was sentenced to eleven years in federal prison for receipt and distribution of child pornography.

Thirty-year-old Jeffrey had been attracted to very young girls for as long as he could remember. Images of young girls entered his mind whenever he thought of sex and he compulsively masturbated to thoughts of them almost every day. He did not want to do this, but felt compelled to do so. He wished he was attracted to adult women, but he was not. In despair, he attempted to hang himself in his parents' closet. Eventually he discovered child pornography on the internet. He was caught, and the judge sentenced him to ten years in federal prison.

Each of the men risked having other inmates learn of their offenses; each of them wanted to change their live. We all saw our program as way to learn to change.

Wally led the early program with a Bible study on grace, the unmerited help and forgiveness that God gives to those who ask. Wally had a deep love of God and incredible knowledge of the Bible. He knew the prison rules and knew the inmates. After a few weeks Wally recruited Simon, a former sex offender who had ministered to other sex offenders for fifteen years. Simon also had a deep love of God, plus he knew what it was like to be a sex offender and recover. Wally was more a talker, Simon a listener. They made a great team.

The program went well, but not always smoothly. Our program had a simple rule, copied from an ad for Las Vegas: "What happens in Vegas stays in Vegas." Confidentiality was critical to a program that allowed us to speak honestly about what we had done, breaking the secrecy of our addiction. One of our participants, Brian, who was small, afraid, and insecure, broke the anonymity when threatened and told the "haters" which inmates attended our meetings. Some of our participants were then threatened, and some stopped coming. New members became hard to find. Brian was shipped to another prison. The group continued.

We tried to focus the group on recovery, on learning what we needed to do to change our lives and not reoffend, but the group also gave us the opportunity to speak out about persecution in our housing units or elsewhere in the prison. When other criminals refuse to associate with you because they think your crime is worse than theirs, when they get up from the chow hall table when you sit down, when they call you garbage and scum, it is painful. Even when you know that those behaviors are only happening because the attacker is so ashamed, and feels so badly about himself that he's striking out, it still hurts and can be frightening. God asks us to love our enemy, but loving your enemy can be really tough. The group became a place to discuss those hurts and fears. We did our best to forgive and love all our neighbors.

We also were able to talk about the perceived inequities in the justice system. Men who were guilty and caught breaking the law found it necessary to complain: "They arrested me at work in front of my coworkers after they told me they would arrest me at home" or "They arrested me at home and handcuffed me in front of my children after I had agreed to turn myself in." We complained about our sentences. "How come you got five years and I got fifteen for the same crime?" "My plea bargain called for probation, but the judge sentenced me to ten years." We were terrified about the challenges we would face leaving prison – sex offender registration, laws restricting where we could live or where we could travel, restrictions on computer use, how we could get jobs – and we needed to talk about those things also. Would we be able to live with our children? We felt fear, anger, and anxiety about things we could not change, about things we could not predict.

Slowly we learned we could not un-ring the bell of the past; a pickle can never again become a cucumber. The future was not ours to control. With God's help we could manage today if we put aside our guilt and shame about the past and our fears of tomorrow. We can only live successfully in today, taking one day at a time.

Mostly we focused on recovery, on learning how not to reoffend. We read several books on how sex addiction works in our brains and how to counteract its power. Then we tried one of the Christian twelve-step programs. Wally asked me to lead the program, and I changed the focus from a broad program for all addictions to one specifically for sex offenders. The program combined twenty-six short lessons, Bible study, and the twelve steps of recovery, showing how to strengthen our relationship with God.

After completing the program in a year, we affiliated with Sex Addicts Anonymous, one of the international twelve-step sex addiction programs that encourage participants to seek their Higher Power, the God of their understanding. We continued using the twelve steps as the focus of our spiritual recovery program. Men who had committed the most offensive crimes were learning to love God. That was the outcome of God's message to Wally. After five years, we had a solid and growing core of men committed to learning and living as God wanted.

CHAPTER 25

Recovery and the Twelve Steps

TWELVE-STEP PROGRAMS GREW FROM A conversation between Bill W. and Dr. Bob in 1934. Bill Wilson, an alcoholic travelling for business, was craving a drink. If he were to abstain, he knew he needed to talk with another alcoholic—someone who understood his struggle. He met with Dr. Bob, told him his story, and never took another drink. Dr. Bob took a last drink June 10, 1935, and this is considered the origin of Alcoholics Anonymous (AA).[xxviii]

The program of Alcoholics Anonymous has grown nationally and internationally since then; it now claims more than two million members. Addicts have formed other fellowships modeled on the methodology, literature, traditions, community, and culture of AA, including at least five programs for sex addicts. The program of Sex Addicts Anonymous uses these twelve steps as guidelines for recovery:

THE TWELVE STEPS OF SEX ADDICTS ANONYMOUS

1. We admitted we were powerless over addictive sexual behavior – that our lives had become unmanageable.
2. Came to believe that a Power greater than ourselves could restore us to sanity.
3. Made a decision to turn our will and our lives over to the care of God as we understood God.
4. Made a searching and fearless moral inventory of ourselves.

5. Admitted to God, to ourselves, and to another human being the exact nature of our wrongs.
6. Were entirely ready to have God remove all these defects of character.
7. Humbly asked God to remove our shortcomings.
8. Made a list of all persons we had harmed and became willing to make amends to them all.
9. Made direct amends to such people wherever possible, except when to do so would injure them or others.
10. Continued to take personal inventory and when we were wrong promptly admitted it.
11. Sought through prayer and meditation to improve our conscious contact with God as we understood God, praying only for knowledge of God's will for us and the power to carry that out.
12. Having had a spiritual awakening as a result of these steps, we tried to carry this message to other sex addicts and to practice these principles in our lives.[2]

Recovery can be understood as a spiritual process in which the addict repairs his broken thinking; he replaces his faulty beliefs with healthy new ones. The twelve-step programs I attended gave me critical guidance. At the suggestion of twelve-step programs, early on in recovery I built my relationship with my Higher Power, which for me, as a Christian, is God. Accepting that I had failed to make good decisions on my own, I recognized that God could provide Good Orderly Direction in my life. I learned to let God make my decisions for me, and to do things according to what I believed was God's way. I learned to admit the damage I had caused, to forgive myself, and to forgive others. I tried to make things right with those I had hurt. As I did this, I experienced a return of my personal integrity; I

---

[2] International Service Organization of SAA, Inc., 2005, pp 20.21. Other twelve-step programs use slightly different adaptations of the twelve steps. Sexaholics Anonymous refers to lust rather than addictive sexual behavior in Step 1. The author does not mean to suggest a preference.

found a new feeling of purpose; and I began living a healthy life, free from sexual addiction.

Although I made bad decisions that led me toward addiction, I had not chosen to be a sex addict. In my wildest dreams, I did not imagine that I would develop an uncontrollable, self-destructive passion to look at pictures of children engaged in sexual behavior. I never imagined I would damage my family, lose my career, destroy my relationship with God, or be sentenced to federal prison. I did not imagine the compulsions I would develop to engage in sexual activity in hotel rooms, clubs, and public parks with people I did not know or care about. I did not anticipate the injury that would poison my mind every day for too many decades. Recognition of my powerlessness over the development of my addiction, as suggested in Step One of the twelve-step programs, **"We admitted we were powerless over addictive sexual behavior -- that our lives had become unmanageable,"** has helped me let go of the crushing shame that came as my denial was stripped away.

When I was a child I could not meet my own needs; I needed help. We all do. Disappointed in the help I received from my family and peers, I learned not to trust their help. Over time, I learned to refuse help from others. But whatever strengths that I had, they were not enough to protect me from myself. In recovery, I am learning to take responsibility, to ask for God's help and the help of other recovering addicts, in order to make good decisions. Step Two, **"Came to believe that a Power greater than ourselves could restore us to sanity,"** suggests this work. I may not have been responsible for developing my disease, but I am responsible for my recovery, and for asking for help when I am up against my limitations.

During the years of my active addiction, I had an illusion of control. I thought I could handle things, and because I thought I could handle my problems, I kept having those problems over and over again. Trying to control my addiction only made it worse. I have learned about a paradox: the only way I can begin to gain control over my addiction is to acknowledge that I cannot control it. I had to surrender and ask for help from God and others, as suggested in Step Three, **"Made a decision to turn our will and our life over to the care of God, as we understand God."**

I asked for help at the treatment center from the staff and other addicts. I asked for help in recovery groups and began to trust the judgment of others in recovery. I asked for help in prison. I broke the power that secrecy held over my life by talking with others openly about my problems. There is a risk involved in honesty; many in our society do not want to hear open discussion about sex, much less about sexual addiction. Some laugh and see sexual addiction as funny, minimizing the potential damage. Others judge us, criticize us, and view us as monsters. In prison there was danger of harassment and even violence in talking about sex addiction. For those of us who grew up learning that others could not be trusted, building trust is a slow process. But speaking out, learning to trust, and asking for help are essential for recovery.

I recognized that if I did not have the power to control my addiction I needed to turn to a power greater than myself. For me that power was God. I had already decided to bring God into my life. I came to believe that even though I had distanced myself from God, God had never been far from me. I've met a few addicts who believe that all they have to do is ask God to cure their addiction and "poof," they will no longer be addicts. I don't doubt that God can do that, but I know that's not how God has chosen to handle it for me. In my case I had asked God many times to take away my addiction: I believe He answered that prayer by sending a team of armed FBI agents to my door. I was not grateful for that at the time. I am now. Nothing short of that was likely to have had an impact on me.

When I asked Him to take away my sex addiction, first He had to attract my attention. Then He showed me what I had to do. God will do His part, but I need to do mine. I had made the mistake of asking but not listening. I had asked God to do His part, but I did not ask God what He expected of me. The twelve steps gave me other effective guidelines for my recovery.

I learned that my addiction was more than compulsive sexual behavior; it involved distorted thinking, mistaken beliefs, and inappropriate emotions. I used the fourth step of recovery: **"Made a searching and fearless moral inventory of ourselves"** to address these issues. I reviewed my resentments, the anger I held inside of me for events long past. I began to understand the fears I had of the future. I listed each of the people I had hurt. As I did my inventory I began to understand my responsibility in the development of my personal problems and what I could do to improve my relationships. Although there were elements beyond my control that led me to develop my addiction, I am an adult. I accepted that my behavior was my responsibility and my recovery required my participation. Early in recovery I learned to build an experience of support with others in the recovery community. Now, I learned to address my particular patterns of relating that created problems for myself and others. With the help of my sponsor, I looked inside myself and identified those things that needed to be changed. I listed and accepted the character defects that had been underlying my addiction.

Taking the next step, Step 5: **"Admitted to God, to ourselves, and to another human being the exact nature of our wrongs,"** began in a way that was surprisingly easy for me. I had handled admitting what I had done wrong to myself when I went through the process of honestly writing down my wrongs, one at a time. I had very specifically listed the exact nature of my wrongs. While before I had denied, to myself, much of the harm I had done, now I faced it head on. I trusted that God was already totally aware of my sins, that He loved me no matter what I had done. I got down on my knees, let Him know that I was aware of them too, and asked His forgiveness. I knew it would be granted.

Admitting my sinful behavior to another human being was more daunting. Trust is hard to come by in prison. My sponsor was a good man, and I trusted him. He had been in recovery from sex addiction for several years and from alcohol for twenty-five. He has worked the steps with his sponsor. Even so, I was saying out loud every example I could remember of dishonest, harmful, and disgusting illegal behavior to another inmate. It was a long list.

I listed all my resentments, what caused them, and what part of me was hurt or threatened by them. Did they affect my self-esteem, my pride, my emotional security, my ambitions, my relationships, or my finances? Where was I to blame? Was I selfish, dishonest, self-seeking, inconsiderate, or afraid? I was very specific as I answered each question.

I listed my fears. What am I afraid of? Why am I afraid? What part of me have I been relying on that has failed me? Was it my self-reliance, self-confidence, self-discipline, or self-will? What part of me does the fear affect? Identifying my fears was difficult, but I patiently took the time to complete the task.

I reviewed my sex conduct – the who's and what's, the exact nature of what I did wrong. Did I arouse jealousy, bitterness, or suspicion? Who did I harm? What should I have done instead? I did not want to answer those questions, but I did.

I made a long list of the people I had harmed, to the best of my ability. What did I do, or fail to do, that caused the harm? Which of my attitudes and defects caused me to do things that harmed someone else? What is the exact nature of my wrongs? I asked again: Was I selfish, dishonest, self-seeking, or inconsiderate? Was I afraid? Did I lack self-discipline or self-control? Was I playing God, trying to control other people? Was my ego involved? What were the consequences? What should I have done instead?

Sitting on a couch in the prison chapel, my sponsor listened politely, never judging. How could someone listen to all the garbage of my life and not judge? Instead, at times he gave examples of how he had done the same things or felt the same way. As I shared my secrets, the most painful part of myself, my shame and isolation abated, and again I felt a huge weight was lifted from my shoulders. I shared with him the defects I had identified in my character; he gently added a few. As I finished, we fell to our knees in prayer. I could feel the experience of God in my life.

After I finished, I returned to my room and sat quietly, reviewing the past few hours. Had I left anything out? I thanked God for what had just happened – an experience I knew would change my life. Was I willing for God to remove every one of those defects of character that we had identified? Without any doubt, I was. I could not change by myself; I needed to change, and I needed God. I had completed Step 6: **"Were entirely ready to have God remove all these defects of character."**

Character defects, however, do not disappear simply because we acknowledge them. When I had asked God to remove my sex addiction, I was asking Him to remove the symptoms, like a man with lung cancer asking God to take away the cough. That didn't work. I needed God to show me how to lose the anger, the resentment, and the fear. I needed God to help me give away my pride, self-centeredness, arrogance, and the multitude of other character defects I have accumulated over my life, defects blocking me from being spiritually connected to others, so I could become the man He wants me to be. Then, being better connected to others, perhaps, my addiction would go into remission. After dinner I met my sponsor again and together, on our knees, we prayed aloud the following prayer from the book *Alcoholics Anonymous*:

> My Creator, I am now willing that you should have all of me, good and bad. I pray that you now remove from me every single defect of character that stands in the way of my usefulness to you and my fellows. Grant me strength, as I go out from here, to do your bidding. Amen.

I had completed Step 7: **"Humbly asked God to remove our shortcomings."**

I began speaking regularly with God, with a fervor I had never had before, and I listened to Him carefully. God did not always speak directly – sometimes He spoke through others – but I heard His message. God asked me to forgive those I believed had hurt me. I had carried anger and resentment inside me for most of my life: anger at my parents, anger at my peers who abused me as a child, anger at my bosses who saw the future of their organization differently than I did, anger at my wife and her depression. That anger had given me permission to act out, to look at pornography. Only by forgiving them could I relieve my anger.

Years before, when I was visiting South Korea, I had stopped at a small park called Independence Park. In that park was a statue dedicated to forgiving the Japanese for all the atrocities they had committed against Korea. On each side of the statue, one side in Korean, the other in English, they listed every horror, every resentment, and then forgave them. At the time I thought the horrors were listed so they would not forget them, but I now realize that to forgive, I needed to identify and list those things I was forgiving. That was the only way I could end the resentment and heal the anger I felt. Hanging onto anger was selfish and stood in the way of letting God guide my life.

Forgiveness would cost me nothing except my pride. So, I began, slowly and imperfectly, to forgive those I believed had hurt me.

I found some were easy to forgive. I had inherited my father's workaholism and recognized that it came from the effects of the Great Depression in his life; I forgave him without difficulty. I had never expressed appreciation for the affluence and privileged lifestyle in which I was raised, for which he was responsible, but I began to experience gratitude. The offense of the boys who abused me on the playground and in the shower came from children who were struggling to find their own way. They did not imagine the effect their actions might have on my life. The man who abused me in the woods suffered from an illness he did not know how to cure. My boss had the right to lead the organization in his way; his decisions were not directed at me. My wife brought her depression with her from childhood.

I struggled most with forgiving my mother, but finally recognized that she was the product of her own background. I try to remind myself that most people, no matter how bad their behavior seems, are doing the best they can at the time. Sometimes looking in a mirror helps; when I recognize my own limitations, I can be more forgiving of others. Mother had done the best she could.

My most difficult challenge was forgiving myself. I had been a battleground of anger, resentment, self-centeredness, and self-hatred. I had split myself into two, divided myself into compartments – one who objectified others, used child pornography, and separated himself from God; the other was a perfectionist who judged and condemned all those things and found himself deficient, unacceptable, and corrupt. It was only by accepting that neither of these compartments was the place that God wanted me to be that I could forgive myself, and bring those two warring sides into one.

Step 8 suggests, **"Make a list of all persons we had harmed and become willing to make amends to them all."** I began with the lists I had compiled when I did my personal inventory. As an adult, I had hurt many people. When I was active in my addiction I had separated myself from my wife, my children, and my grandchildren, and had failed to be a responsible husband, parent, and grandparent. Moving to top management of any corporation involves almost total commitment and partnership of the husband, wife, and family. Our roots ended up in my profession instead of the community, and our connections to those we worked with instead of our neighbors. When I was arrested, the pain of my arrest affected not only my marriage, but the entire structure on which Ellyn and I had built our lives. Our income was diminished; friendships were shattered. My children lost a father who could be involved in their lives, my grandchildren lost a grandparent. People looked at Ellyn as if the crimes were hers. They, too, experienced shame, confusion, and judgment. My employer was hurt, and my coworkers. My church and its pastor were hurt. The damage I caused was excessive, and my list was extensive, but I was not done.

Of course, the youth in the pictures were hurt. They did not know me, did not even know I possessed images of them. But by viewing the pictures of their abuse I was encouraging the industry that supported their abuse and that of others. The number of my victims continued to grow. I'm sure there are others I have not yet identified and perhaps never will.

As a recovering addict, I now felt an obligation to make amends, to attempt to right the wrong I have done to so many. It's not enough to recognize the hurt I have caused, the resentments I have been part of, the anger that radiated from me to those around me. God asks that I attempt to repair the damage that I have done, and to prepare myself to serve God and others. I will never recover from my sex addiction, and I will never have peace and serenity in the present, until I have done the best I can to make up for my poor behavior. Step 9 says: **"Make direct amends to such people wherever possible, except when to do so would injure them or others."**

I attempted to meet personally in the prison visiting room with as many of the people I had harmed as possible. My approach was straightforward and simple. First I prayed, asking God for his guidance. I consulted with my sponsor. Then I called the people I had harmed and asked for a meeting. Until I left prison my list would be limited to the few who could visit me. I began by honestly telling them that I was a sex and pornography addict, and that it was vital to my recovery to make amends to those I had hurt. I was then very specific about what I had done that hurt them. I made no excuses and placed no blame on them. I acknowledged that my actions had consequences. I simply took responsibility for my part in the harm. I let them know my character defects involved. For example, I might say, "I was selfish, dishonest, and afraid." I took responsibility for my actions, invited them to tell me any additional ways I had harmed them, and then quietly listened to their answer. If there were specific things I expected to do to make things right, I listed them. I concluded by asking if there were other things they expected of me.

I was not responsible for their reaction; I was only responsible for doing the best I could in owning my own part. Most people were kind and respectful, glad that I had begun the effort to make things right. In some cases, my amends led to a renewed relationship on honest footing. In other cases, the relationship would never again become what it had been. Nonetheless, the person may have felt better because I had approached them and made the amend. Regardless of their response, it mattered that I had done my part.

There were others to whom I owed amends that I could not approach. Some amends would have to wait until I left prison; others could only be made through prayer. Some had moved away, or I had never known them personally at all. How do I make these amends? I cannot change the past. My parents had died years ago. Sometime later, after leaving prison, I made amends to my parents at the cemetery where they were buried, which was a very moving experience for me. But I can't contact the youth in the pictures I viewed. The images I looked at are still embedded in my brain like a video library. I must avoid replaying them, however, lest I trigger a relapse. One amend is donating any proceeds from the sale of this book to organizations that help abused children. Others will be more difficult.

I would be separated from my family for seven years. How do I replace those years? I have apologized, but that is not enough. No, I must repent, turn from the sin of my past and change how I behave today and in the future, making a living amends with new behavior. The most important thing I can do is not repeat behavior that harmed others.

I can and must tell those I hurt of my sorrow and my commitment, and I have done that, wherever possible. But words have less meaning now, because the trust has been damaged. I made amends to my children, and when the two youngest said, "Stop, Dad, that's enough," I thought I was through. I didn't realize how much longer it would take to make amends to my oldest, the one who bore my name.

In some instances, trust will only be rebuilt when people see the changes in my life, when it becomes clear that I am living differently. Changing the opinion of others is out of my control. I can only do the best I can, and leave the rest to God. What is it then that I do to change my life?

Certainly, I abstain from those behaviors that were part of my addiction. I don't look at pornography, not only in the legal sense, but I also abstain from looking at any pictures, films, television shows, books, or magazines that may encourage me to objectify or fantasize. But recovery for me is not only what I don't do, it is also what I must do. I must pray and listen to God, and those times when I do so become a highlight of my day. God always knew me, and in my recovery, I have grown to know and trust Him. I hadn't realized that God was that big. I go to church and recovery meetings, and I speak to other recovering addicts every day. I fill my time with healthy behaviors: exercise, reading and study, spending time with friends, writing, helping others, and rebuilding my relationship with Ellyn. It is the presence of these positive acts that removes my addictive thinking and brings me security and joy.

It is generally not wise for a recovering addict to trust himself. That's one reason we are encouraged to have sponsors. They are mentors and partners who hold us accountable; they teach us from what they have learned from their own experience. In twelve-step programs we say that a sponsor should have depth and weight. They have engaged in the same addictive behavior that I have, and they don't do it anymore. They have recovered from the same illness that I have, and they now help others to recover. I have had several guides in my recovery. Roy sponsored me before I went to prison and has now been sober from sex addiction for over twenty years. Al sponsored me and many other men by mail while I was in prison. Pat, an accountability partner and fellow inmate, completed his sentence and went home. I doubt I could have entered recovery without them.

While in prison I served as a sponsor to several men who desired recovery. Edward and I met four days each week at 7 a.m. Edward had dropped out of

Cal-Berkeley and worked as an EMT for a local ambulance service. We sat on one of the benches in the middle of the prison park and watched the brilliant sunrise beyond a double-topped oak tree and a fence beyond. I listened as he disclosed the defects in his life, and we talked about apology, forgiveness, and the power of God to change our lives. Edward went home to California, has a good job, is active in his church, and continues to attend recovery meetings regularly.

Frank and I walked on the road around the park, stopping occasionally to feed peanuts to the squirrels that lived in the large oak trees, as Frank talked about his addiction to bondage and adultery, and about the hurt he brought into the life of his ex-wife and daughter. Six-foot-two and two hundred pounds, Frank worked as a state policeman for twenty years. Forced into early retirement for sexually harassing a subordinate, he bounced from job to job: bus driver, fast-food restaurant manager, and water department supervisor. When Frank arrived in prison he was desolate. All hope and joy in his life was gone, and he could find nothing good in anything he had ever done. As he talked, listened, and attended meetings, he saw that God would give him the power to change his future. Frank went home, first to a homeless shelter, then to an inexpensive motel, and finally to purchase his own home. He has a job, he has reconciled with his adult daughter, he does volunteer construction work for the poor, and he leads recovery meetings at his church. The desolation is gone, replaced by joy and gratitude. He is not the same man he used to be.

For some recovery is more difficult than for others. Some addicts don't want to recover; they just want to stop acting out their deviant behavior. After they stop acting out, they still have the same addictive temperament and self-centered righteousness they had before; they've just quit acting out. In recovery programs we call it white-knuckling, and for most people that doesn't work very well in the long run.

Young, tall and slender, with long chestnut hair, Toby had owned a small-town restaurant. Injured in a car accident, he walked with a limp. As we stood by a stone wall at the edge of the park, Toby was anxious to tell his story. I listened without judgment. But Toby could not forgive those who let him down – his father, his ex-wife – and he fell back into his depression. He could not change himself, so he changed his surroundings, bouncing from one prison job to another, changing religions frequently, eventually transferring to another institution. We are each responsible for our own recovery. Some do better than others.

I could not change the past. I learned that what I could do was the next right thing today; take the next steps, one at a time. My future remained in front of me, in the hands of God. Even in prison, I learned gratitude: I learned to want what I have today.

The twelve-step programs gave me critical healing, guidance, and support. The promises of Alcoholics Anonymous, based on the experience of the early members, read:

> We are going to know a new freedom and a new happiness. We will not regret the past nor wish to shut the door on it. We will comprehend the word serenity and we will know peace. No matter how far down the scale we have gone we will see how our experience will benefit others. That feeling of uselessness and self-pity will disappear. We will lose interest in selfish things and gain interest in our fellows. Self-seeking will slip away. Our whole attitude and outlook upon life will change. Fear of people and economic insecurity will leave us. We will intuitively know how to handle situations, which used to baffle us. We will suddenly realize that God is doing for us what we could not do for ourselves.[xxix]

Many individuals in recovery even develop gratitude for their disease, for bringing them into the recovery way of life.

CHAPTER 26

Going Home

When it came time to leave prison, I remembered the many communities where I had lived and worked before. I was coming to see prison as just one more stop, one more experience in my life. Like every other place I had lived, I had met people in prison I would never forget: drug dealers, bank robbers, money launderers, sex offenders. Most were guilty of committing serious felonies. I believe a few were innocent, convicted by a jury and an overly aggressive prosecutor. Although I don't condone their crimes, many of them had become my friends. Others I hope never to see again. I believe God doesn't give me only the people I want, He gives me the people I need to help me, hurt me, leave me, love me, and make me the person He wants me to be.

As my release date grew closer, I knew that most of all I would miss my recovery group. Sex offenders in our prisons live a life of fear. On arriving at prison, we are told to keep our crime a secret. The security concerns are real. Many of us are discovered to be sex offenders, "outed" to the prison population, and harassed both verbally and physically. Yet the fear and secrecy are two of the very pressures that hold sex offenders in their addiction to compulsive sexual behavior. It is crucial to be open and honest in order to experience recovery. The following are my comments to the recovery group before leaving prison.

My name is Brady. Welcome to this meeting.

I'm going to begin this meeting a little differently than usual, with a story from Spanish poet Juan Ramon Jimenez. The story is about the author and his little donkey, Platero. Listen closely.

Dressed in mourning, with my long black beard and small black hat, I must look odd riding on Platero's grey softness. When, on my way to the vineyards, I cross the last streets, whitewashed and dazzling bright in the sunlight, shaggy haired gypsy children, clothed in green, red, and yellow rags, run after us shrilling a long, drawn-out call: "CRAZY MAN, CRAZY MAN!"

Before us lies the open country. Face to face with the vast pure sky of fiery blue, my eyes – so far from my ears – open contentedly, receiving in all its quietness that nameless calm, that harmonious and divine serenity that lies in the infinitude of the horizon. And from a distance, over the fields, sharp cries, finely muffled, broken, breathless, faint: "Crazy man, crazy man."[xxx]

Now close your eyes for a minute. Can you see the angry inmate running down the hall after you? You've seen him before, shrilling a long, drawn-out call: "CHILD MOLESTER! CHILD MOLESTER!"
Before us, too, lies the open country. We can watch, across the fields, the brilliant reds and oranges of a sunset, our eyes – so far from our ears – can open contentedly, and even here in prison we can receive that harmonious and divine serenity that God will give us, if only we ask and believe.
And now, from a distance, the sharp cries are muffled, broken, breathless, and so faint we can barely hear them: "Child molester, child molester."
Please join me in the serenity prayer:

God, grant me the serenity
to accept the things I cannot change,
courage to change the things I can,
and wisdom to know the difference.

This meeting has provided us the opportunity to talk about those things that are going on in the prison. Hatred, harassment, and theft have all been on our agenda – things that made, and still make, our life here difficult.

This meeting has provided us the opportunity to complain about the unfairness of the justice system: long sentences that will cause some of us to spend more time in prison for looking at child pornography than some inmates get for murder. Sentences that are far longer in the federal system than they are in most states. We've talked about the lack of integrity among prosecutors and the police, who told us one thing and did another.

We've talked about our fears of the difficulties we will face when leaving prison: sex offender registration, limits on where we can live, who we can see, limits on computer use, the difficulty we expect to find in getting a job.

Let me tell you another story. A college professor came to class one day with a large, wide-mouth jar. He put some fist-sized rocks into the jar until no more would fit. He asked the class if the jar was full, and they agreed that it was.

The professor took a bag of gravel from under his desk and poured it into the jar until the gravel had reached the top. He asked again if the jar was full. The class was not so sure any more. The professor poured a bag of sand into the jar, and it filtered down among the gravel. The professor again asked if the jar was full. The class was on to him now, and expected more. The professor emptied a pitcher of water into the jar, until the jar was full up to the top. Finally, everyone agreed the jar was full.

Then the professor asked what the moral of the story was. A student answered, "There is always time for you to give us one more assignment." The professor said, "No. The moral of the story is, if you don't put the big rocks in first, they'll never fit in at all."

It's okay for you and me to talk about the challenges of living in prison. It's okay to talk about our anger at the justice system, and our fear of the difficulties we'll face leaving prison. But my advice is to let those on the outside worry about the things we cannot change. There's nothing we can do about them in here, and worrying about them gets in the way of our recovery. What's really important is that we learn how to change our lives, so that when we leave here we don't come back, so that we become the person God wants us to be. Those are the big rocks and where we should spend the bulk of our time.

Listen to the words from Jeremiah 29: 11-13.

"For I know the plans I have for you," declares the Lord, "plans to prosper you and not to harm you, plans to give you hope and a future. Then you will call upon me and come and pray to me, and I will listen to you. You will seek me and find me when you seek me with all your heart."[xxxi] (NIV Study Bible, 1995)

God has plans to give us hope and a future. Trust Him.

Most of us in this group are suffering from an addiction. We were doing something we knew was wrong, yet we were unable to stop. Let me describe for you again how addiction works:

Our addiction cycle begins with a trigger – an uncomfortable thought, an argument with a girlfriend, a beautiful person on television – that creates an uncomfortable emotion and leads to anxiety. We begin obsessing about something pleasurable, sexual fantasies to hide the anxiety. We enter into a ritual, a trance that's so unconscious that it doesn't interrupt the obsessions, the fantasies. We turn on the computer and go to a chat room, or we drive to an adult video store, or we stare lustfully at a woman, whatever that ritual is for you. And eventually we act out – maybe we masturbate, or we have sex with a stranger, or we visit a prostitute, or we touch a child. Then we feel ashamed, and we become anxious, and the fantasies begin again, and we can't stop.

There are some who believe that all we have to do to stop is to ask God to take away our addiction, and "poof," it will be gone. That wasn't the way it worked for me. I could go to church in the morning and be looking at porn in the afternoon. God sent a dozen armed F.B.I. agents to my door to attract my attention. Most of you have heard my story: a high-ranking person with significant public profile caught trading child pornography on the internet and engaging in sexual activity with strangers I did not know or care about. I needed to change my life, and I didn't know how.

Following my arrest, I went to a private residential treatment center for four and a half months and began my recovery. The professionals there quoted from the "Big Book" of Alcoholics Anonymous: "Abandon yourself to God…. Admit your faults to Him and to your fellows. Clear away the wreckage of your past. Give freely of what you find."[xxxii]

My dream is that you too can recover from your addiction.

When I used child pornography I believed that I was committing a victimless crime and I minimized my part in the harm being done to children. I have since learned that many of the children pictured relate being haunted by shame, embarrassment, and guilt throughout their lifetime. They worry that someone will recognize their image and attempt to contact them. Victims whose images are found online experience more depression and anxiety than other sexually abused children.[xxxiii] Sexual addiction is a disease that brings harm to the addict and to others as well. I regret the damage I have done and hope to make amends for that damage.

Before my arrest, my mind was imprisoned by the obsessions and fantasies of my addiction. For the past seven years, my body has been imprisoned by the steel walls and concertina wire surrounding this prison, but my mind has been free.

From Psalm 107, verses 10 through 16, I read:

Some sat in darkness and deepest gloom,
prisoners suffering in iron chains,
for they had rebelled against the words of God
and despised the counsel of the Most High.

That was me.

So he submitted them to bitter labor;
they stumbled and there was no one to help.
They cried to the lord in their trouble,
and he saved them from their distress.
He brought them out of darkness and the deepest gloom
and broke away their chains.

That's what happened to me.

Let them give thanks to the Lord for his unfailing love
and his wondrous deeds for men,

for he breaks down gates of bronze
and cuts through bars of iron.

When I entered treatment, I was told that in recovery I would no longer regret my past – the self-hatred and shame I carried because of my addictive behavior would disappear. The anger I held through memories of childhood abuse would fade away. The regret I had at the destruction I had brought upon myself – lost job, destroyed relationships, tattered reputation, and prison – would leave me. I was told I would come to appreciate my past as a gift because of the opportunity it would provide for the future. I was told that although I could not control my addiction, God would. I would find God, and through God would find myself. I was hesitant and skeptical, but I did what was asked of me; looked for God in the events, people, and experiences of my life. And I found a new life I would not have found if not for my addiction.

In a few weeks I'm leaving here, and you will be here to finish your sentence. The most difficult part of prison for me has not been the challenges we face here, it's been the separation from my loved ones. I know how difficult that is for you. Yet here is my advice for you: put the bitterness behind you. In simple words, grow right here in this prison, where you are planted. Do not waste the time God has given you in prison.

I encourage you to live one day at a time. Your past is gone and cannot be undone. You can't un-ring the bell. Your future will come in its own time; worrying will not make it better. Today is yours. Today, with the sun of each new dawn, is yours.

My friend Bruce recently asked me if I thought being in prison was part of God's plan for my life. I don't think God put me in prison. I don't think the FBI agents, or the prosecutor, or the judge put me in prison. I put myself in prison. But I believe if God didn't want me in prison, I wouldn't be here. What I know today with certainty is that while I was here, God entered my life in a way that seems miraculous, and that He is doing things in my life that I was unable to do for myself. I went to prison because God loved me.

And now, after seven years, I'm going home in seventeen days. My wife and children will meet me at the gate. Someday, you will go home too. I have no delusions. I know that in many ways my departure will be easier than for some of you. I have income and don't need a job. I have a home and family to go to. Some of you do not. I have a church home that has written and welcomed me. But I also face obstacles that you will face – sex offender registration, probation and counseling, limits on computer use, and other unknown challenges every convicted sex offender faces. I have not been shielded from temptation in here, and I know there will be even more temptation on the outside.

Poet Edna St. Vincent Millay wrote these lines:

Two men looked out their prison bars,
one saw mud, the other stars.

I see stars. You can too.

Here's what Juan Ramon Jimenez, the crazy man, said about the locked gate in his small Spanish town of Moguer:

Whenever I went to the Diezmo store, I would always return along the wall on San Antonio Street and stop at the locked grilled gate leading to the open country. I would place my face against the bars and look to the right and to the left, straining my eyes eagerly as far as my sight could reach. From its very threshold, worn and lost in the nettles and mallows, a path starts and disappears, downgrade, at Angustias. And below its hedge, there is a wide low road that I have never traveled….

What a magical fascination it was to see, through the iron squares of the gate, the selfsame landscape and sky outside it. It was as though a roof and wall of illusion separated this particular view from the rest, to leave it alone behind the closed grill. And I could see the highway, with its bridge and its smoke poplars, and the brick kiln, and the Palos Hills, and the steamers of Huelva, and, at nightfall, the lights of Riotinto wharf, and the tall and lonely eucalyptus tree of Arroyos against the purple of the fading sunset….

> The storekeepers used to tell me, laughing, that the gate was not locked…In my dreams, the gate opened to the most prodigious gardens, into the most marvelous fields…time and again I went of a morning to the gate convinced that I would find behind it what my imagination added – I do not know whether consciously or unconsciously – to reality…

I am reminded of peering down from the recreation yard and seeing the Interstate highway with cars and trucks and people traveling freely; and over there the downtown of the city with its majestic skyscrapers. Down the hill are the beautiful churches with towering steeples, and over here children playing soccer. I could hear the whistles of the trains I wanted to be on. And now I'm going through that locked gate, and in my imagination can see the prodigious gardens and the most marvelous fields and the wide, low road that I have not yet traveled.

I have often shared with you communication from our former members and former inmates who are already living the joy and happiness that I expect to find. Frank, who has a job, has reconciled with his daughter and purchased a home, is leading a recovery program in his church, is doing volunteer construction work for the needy, and is experiencing joy and happiness that he has never felt before. Richard, who recently called my wife, is back with his family and has a job and feels good about life. My friend Adam, who began selling used cars while in a halfway house, now manages a car lot. Evan, who had never had a job for more than four months, has now held a job, paid his own bills, and rented his own apartment for a year and a half. These are people like us, who sat in this room. If they found a future, there is a future for you and me too.

In the fourth chapter of Paul's letter to the Philippians, verse 13, he tells me: "I can do anything God asks me to with the help of Christ who gives me the strength and power." With God as my guide, how can I lack confidence in the future?

I end my evening prayer each night this way:

God, take my will and my life,
Guide me in my recovery,
Show me how to live.

I dream that God will do that for you also. Being part of this group has been a great joy. You have made my recovery possible. I will never forget you, and you will continue to be in my prayers. God bless you all.

TIME TO LEAVE

I turned the leadership of the recovery group over to a young man I believed would do a great job. My friends threw a party for me, and I gave away most of my possessions – my blanket, my pillow, my alarm clock, my watch, my small calculator, my marking pen, a pair of new tennis shoes, my bathrobe, and the shelf from my locker. These possessions sound like very little in the free world, but in prison they have great value. I went home with my addiction in remission, with my address book, my Bible, my writing, and an old pair of tennis shoes. I also brought seven years of memories, surprisingly, most of them good.

What It's Like Now

CHAPTER 27

Spirituality

RECOVERY LOOKS DIFFERENT FOR EACH person. Some recover, some don't. I only know what worked for me to become sexually sober and free of addictive behavior, and I have tried to share that with you. I have shared my story of being a four-year-old boy asked to expose himself to a stranger, a fifth grader always picked last for sports teams, a high school freshman bullied and abused in the shower after physical education class, and the oldest son of an overbearing, self-absorbed mother and a workaholic father. What if I had grown up watching animals mating on a farm, or with a neighbor lady who regularly exposed herself through her bedroom window, or with a father who raped my sister or molested me? Would my sexual deviations have been different or nonexistent? What if I had grown up in a perfect world with a perfect home? Would I still have become a sex addict? I will never know.

I've believed in God all my life. I was taught to pray as a child and went to Sunday school regularly. Even at that point in my life – late high school, college, early in my career – when I thought I was too busy to go to church, I believed in God. After Ellyn and I were married, we attended church regularly and quickly became leaders in our church. Despite that, I got so far off track that society chose to incarcerate me for seven years in federal prison. For me, believing in God was not enough. I knew of God, but I needed to know God up close and personal. I needed to experience God helping me.

The book *Alcoholics Anonymous* contains many stories of men and women who have recovered from alcoholism. My favorite is titled "Acceptance was the Answer." The author speaks about serenity and trust in God. He writes:

Acceptance is the answer to *all* my problems today. When I am disturbed, it is because I find some person, place, thing, or situation – some fact of my life – unacceptable to me, and I can find no serenity until I accept that person, place, thing, or situation as being exactly the way it's supposed to be at this moment. Nothing, absolutely nothing, happens in God's world by mistake.[xxxiv]

In my old life, I thought that I was always right; whether the discussion was politics, my job, or when to take out the trash, I wanted everyone else to believe in my way or act in my way. I have learned that I don't always know what's best for me, let alone what's best for everyone else. My job today is to do the best I can, the next right thing, leave the results to God, and accept whatever happens. My sponsor shared with me the following story he had heard and often told:

Acceptance

A farmer awoke one morning to find a beautiful white horse in the pasture in front of his house. He had no idea where the horse had come from, but it was one of the most beautiful horses he had ever seen.

His neighbor came by and saw the horse. He said, "That's the most beautiful horse I've ever seen. Isn't it wonderful that that horse is there in your pasture?"

"Maybe it is and maybe it isn't," said the farmer.

The next day the horse was gone.

His neighbor came by again and said, "Isn't it awful that the beautiful white horse has disappeared?"

"Maybe it is and maybe it isn't," said the farmer.

The next day when the farmer awoke there were four gorgeous white horses in his pasture, each as beautiful as the next.

His neighbor came by and said, "Isn't that the most incredible thing? There are four incredibly beautiful horses in your pasture."

"Maybe it is and maybe it isn't," said the farmer.

The next day the farmer's son went out and rode one of the white horses. He was thrown off the horse and broke his leg.

The neighbor came by and said to the farmer, "Isn't it terrible, your son broke his leg riding the beautiful white horse?"

"Maybe it is and maybe it isn't," said the farmer.

The next day the king came by and said to the farmer, "There is a war beginning, and I need to take your four beautiful white horses." And he did.

The neighbor came by and said to the farmer, "What a horrible thing. The king has taken your four beautiful horses."

"Maybe it is and maybe it isn't," said the farmer.

The next day the king came by to draft the farmer's son into the army to go to war. But the son had a broken leg and couldn't go.

His neighbor came by and said to the farmer, "Isn't it a wonderful thing that your son can't go to war?"

"Maybe it is and maybe it isn't," said the farmer.

Victor Frankl survived the Nazi death camps, watching his family and those around him being led into the gas chambers, never knowing when his turn would come. In *Man's Search for Meaning,* he wrote, "It did not matter what we expected from life, but rather what life expected from us" … "Man's search for meaning is the primary motivation in his life."[xxxv] My addiction, my recovery, and my new relationship with God have given me meaning that was missing.

I am very fortunate. So many men and women leaving prison have no family who cares about them; they have little education, no money, no place to live, no church community to return to, and very little hope for the future. On April 13, 2012, I was released from prison. My wife and three sons greeted me at the door and drove me home.

Life since has been good to me. I write, play golf, see my family, and spend time with Ellyn. My family, my neighbors, and my church family all know my story. I am active in my church. I no longer keep secrets. I currently go to four twelve-step meetings every week, sponsor five sex addicts, and help any way I can. Vern is my current sponsor. He's been sober over twelve years. We meet for an hour every week, and I call him on the phone every day. I stay accountable to him to work my program; he holds my feet to the fire. My sobriety continues, one day at a time.

I've shared with you steps one through nine of the twelve steps. Working these steps helped me become sober. Steps 10, 11, and 12 are the steps I need to stay sober.

Step 10 instructs us, **"Continued to take personal inventory and when we were wrong promptly admitted it."** For most of my life I held my anger and resentments inside. Through working the twelve steps, I have learned that resentments are deadly for me. Others may be able to carry resentments, but I cannot. I have learned that although I continue to have defects in my character (albeit less than I had them before) and I continue to make mistakes, I cannot let them fester. At the end of each day I review my interactions with other people, my emotions, and my relationship with God. I talk to my sponsor, or my wife, or my twelve-step group about my failings. I no longer must be right about everything, but I do need to be aware and accountable. I think about whether I have harmed anyone, and if I have, I make plans to make amends. I no longer must wait for years to become accountable; I do it every day and begin the next day with a clean slate.

The eleventh step says, **"Sought through prayer and meditation to improve our conscious contact with God, as we understood God, praying**

only for knowledge of God's will for us and the power to carry that out." Each night when I review the previous day, I honestly look at whether I have been resentful, selfish, dishonest, or afraid. Is there someone to whom I owe an apology? Am I keeping secrets that need to be shared? Was I kind and loving that day, particularly toward my wife Ellyn? Are there things that I could have done better? Did I spend much of the day thinking of myself? What did I do to help someone else today? I do this review in writing to not omit anything. Then I discuss my list with God, asking His forgiveness and listening for any sense of His instructions.

When I get up in the morning, my spiritual practice begins. I read from a daily meditation book. I look at my plans for the day. I pray and ask God what he wants me to do, and then listen quietly. If I find a conflict between what God wants me to do and what I want to do, I do my best to follow God's will rather than my own. I am not perfect at this; I am not cured of my addiction. My addiction remains in remission as long as I stay in fit spiritual condition, and this work helps me to do this. As the day goes on, I try to review what God wants of me and make sure I'm staying on track. I trust what God tells me. When I do that, I am much less likely to do something foolish, and more likely to remain sober.

In my old life, I prayed regularly. But I did not have the confidence that good things would happen as a result of my prayers. Now I have seen good things happen, miracles that did not happen before. In the scope of the larger world, they are little miracles. But in my life those miracles have been huge things: Ellyn staying with me, my sexual addiction becoming dormant, my living a life with honesty and integrity. Today I have faith that God hears my prayers and answers them.

Step 12 suggests, **"Having had a spiritual awakening as a result of these steps, we tried to carry this message to other sex addicts and to practice these principles in our lives."** There are three parts to this step. The first part reminds me that by this point I am a spiritually different person than I was before. For some people this awakening is a sudden experience, perhaps like the one the Apostle Paul had on the road to Damascus, where a "light from heaven flashed around him. He fell to the ground," heard the voice of Jesus, and immediately changed his life. For me it was a more gradual awakening, occurring over a period of time, and then the realization dawned on me quite suddenly, that I had become a different person who had regained power over sexual behavior. That realization happened in such a simple way. I was lying in bed early one morning, thinking about the coming day, when I realized that God was doing for me what I could not do for myself.

The second part of Step 12 reminds me to carry the message to other sex addicts. I don't go into houses of ill repute or the back rooms of pornographic video stores, screaming for people to change their ways. But I let people know what it used to be like for me, what happened, and what my life is like now. Even today I do not fully understand why God chose to bring me back from the destruction I brought on myself and those around me, unless it was so that I could now help others. That is why I wrote this book.

Most often I meet men and women seeking recovery from sex addiction when they come to a twelve step-meeting at the recommendation of a therapist, or after their spouse has thrown them out of the house, after they have been arrested, or they have hit bottom from other events and found our meetings on the internet. If you seek recovery, you will find a directory of places to find help in the appendix of this book.

I also carry the message by participating at meetings, by keeping in contact with other members; sharing my experience, strength, and hope with them; and by providing hope and encouragement. I also serve as a sponsor to other sex addicts. Recovery is a "we" proposition. Those seeking recovery cannot recover alone, and those of us who have become sober don't stay sober by ourselves, either. The saying goes, "We keep what we have by giving it away." I am grateful for the help I have received – and continue to receive – from my sponsors, and grateful for the opportunity to pass it on.

The third part of Step 12 suggests we practice these principles in our lives. I know that if I am to stay sexually sober I also need to stay spiritually connected with God. There are many spiritual principles that I need to practice every day. Honesty, willingness, forgiveness, serenity, responsibility, gratitude, acceptance, integrity, courage, and faith are all principles that guide my life daily, one day at a time.

Thousands of recovering men and women today are sexually sober, no longer acting out compulsively. I am one of them. We stay sober one day at a time by keeping in conscious contact with God, staying active in twelve-step programs, and practicing the spiritual principles every day. We accept that situations in everyday life bring challenges; we can find God's will in those challenges and respond accordingly. We can live a good and worthwhile life, not despite our challenges but because of them.

To those men and women still caught in the web of sex addiction, I have written this book for you, your families, and others seeking a better understanding of the disease of sex addiction. I am concerned about the increasing challenges we all face, given unfettered access to all things sexual on the internet and elsewhere. Sex addiction is a disease. There is a solution. Society at large may not yet understand our addiction, but we can. When an addict treats sex addiction as a disease, the addict can get better and again become a productive member of society. Thousands of men and women have recovered; thousands more can recover with help. We invite you to join us.

My Hope for You

To those men and women recovering from sex addiction or codependence, I hope this book provides support for you on your journey.

To those still engaging in compulsive sexual behaviors: you're suffering. Recovery is possible. And it starts with the first step of surrender.

To family members and others close to those with sex addiction: addiction is a family illness. Encourage treatment for your friend or relative, but most of all get help to find peace for yourself. You will not regret it.

To therapists, researchers, religious leaders, volunteers, legislators, judges, and others in the community trying to provide constructive solutions to the questions related to compulsive sexual behavior, may God bless you and guide you in your critical work.

To the interested public, including the victims of our crimes, those of us recovering from sex addiction do not ask you to excuse the evil of our crimes. We do ask that you not condemn and ostracize us as hopeless, or deny us the opportunity to change.

Each day I pray to be free of sexual compulsion, to follow God's will, and to be of service to humankind, my recovery community, and especially to my wife and children. My journey has been arduous, but today I have integrity. My life is filled with blessings, and I am grateful. The storm of my addiction has passed, and I am living in the calm of serenity.

APPENDIX 1 - DOES TREATMENT WORK?

DEBATES ABOUT REHABILITATION OFTEN INVOLVE political rhetoric ("My opponent is soft on crime") with lots of talk and little empirical evidence. Along with terrorism, sex offenses are at the top of the list of crimes that bring the most public concern. The public is particularly concerned that previous offenders do not reoffend. As a result, exceptional policies have been established toward those who have been convicted of sexual offenses. Isolated instances of dangerous criminals released from prison and taken out of context are presented as "proof" that rehabilitation doesn't work. The results from a few pioneering clinics are dismissed as outliers or self-serving. Where can we find solid data?

Dr. Fred Berlin, director of the Johns Hopkins Sexual Disorder Clinic, which specializes in the treatment of paraphilic disorders, reported on a study of 2,000 patients who had been evaluated at that clinic over a ten-year period. The five-year criminal recidivism rate for sexual offenses by pedophiles, exhibitionists, and sexual aggressors against women was under 10%. Criminal sexual recidivism for treatment-compliant pedophiles was under 3%.[xxxvi]

Dr. Barry Maletzky, a psychiatrist at the University of Oregon, has treated over 8,000 sex offenders over a period of twenty years. Maletsky uses a wide variety of treatments in a program that lasts three to four months. He uses strict measures of success; no patient who shows any deviant arousal or behavior since the completion of treatment is considered successful, nor is any patient who has any new criminal charges involving sexual activity. Of over 6,000 pedophiles treated, 91.7% met Maletzky's criteria for success. He succeeded in treating other paraphilias with high success rates as well: exhibitionism, 95.4%; voyeurism 93.9%; fetishism 94.0%. His most disappointing results were a 75.5% success rate with rapists.[xxxvii]

Other groups report similar success rates, although programs that are not as thorough report less success. Psychologists know that a disorder may have a number of causes and that it is sometimes necessary to try a number of routes to a given outcome. Scientific methods are not always applied to some treatments because the methods to produce the needed evidence have not yet been developed. Therapeutic expertise plays a major role in the success of these programs.[xxxviii] Experts believe that the longer people stay in treatment, the less likely they are to relapse. The effects of treatment seem to be optimized when patients remain in care and monitoring as long as needed, and there are no limits placed on the length of time they can stay.

There is hope that those with deviant arousal patterns can learn to overcome their difficulties. Treatment for sexual pathology is a relatively new field. In 2001 there were fewer than one hundred sex therapists in the United States, and treatment was only available in a limited number of expensive specialty clinics. By 2011 there were some fifteen hundred sex therapists treating compulsive behavior.[xxxix]

A meta-analysis is a complex statistical technique for combining the results of many studies. Dr. R. Karl Hanson of Corrections Research, Public Safety and Emergency Preparedness, Canada, presented the results of his meta-analysis of 95 different studies from the USA, Canada, and Europe, which included more than 31,000 sex offenders.[xl] He answered the question, "What is the probability of the 'typical' sex offender committing another offense?" and looked at factors influencing which offenders would reoffend. The results of his research challenge commonly held beliefs about sexual recidivism.

The first of his conclusions shocked the public consciousness. Most sex offenders released from custody do not reoffend. After fifteen years following their release, 73% of offenders had not been convicted, or even charged, with another sexual offense. Of course not all sex offenses are detected, but convicted sex offenders live under the community microscope. Some of those charged but not convicted are no doubt innocent. Sex offenders reoffend at a significantly lower rate than individuals convicted of other crimes.[xli]

A 2004 study by Andrew Lewis and Karl Hansen, *Sex Offender Recidivism: A Simple Question*, pointed out that all sex offenders are not equally likely to reoffend. First-time offenders are much less likely to reoffend than those with previous convictions (19% versus 37%). Offenders over the age of fifty are less than half as likely to reoffend as those younger than fifty (12% versus 26%). The longer sex offenders remain offense-free following release from custody, the less likely they are to reoffend.[xlii] Statistical data shows that different types of offenders reoffend at different rates; rapists reoffend at a much higher rate than incest offenders, and offenders who molest boys reoffend at a higher rate than those who molest girls. Most important (in this author's opinion), offenders who complete a treatment program are much less likely to reoffend. Hanson's 2002 study found only a 10% recidivism rate among sex offenders who completed treatment.[xliii] It is important to note that 90% of sex offenders who completed a credible treatment program were not accused or convicted of another sex crime.[xliv]

Current policies in the United States intended to prevent repeat offenses by sex offenders include lengthy prison sentences, probation as long as lifetime, and public sex offender registration for the rest of the offender's life. Offenders are often not allowed to live near parks, schools, swimming pools, or even bus stops, despite empirical knowledge that where the offender lives has no relation to where he commits his crime. State and local policies in some locations include "Sexual Predator" signs in front of the offender's home, special license plates on his car, "Sex Offender" printed on his driver's license, and more. These restrictions affect not only the offender but also his or her family. Some communities simply outlaw sex offenders from living in the community at all.

These are not easy issues to discuss. The public is outraged at the number of sex crimes. Sex offenses are damaging, heinous crimes, and any possibility of a sex offender reoffending brings feelings of anger and fear, and rightfully so. Yet the United States already has the largest number of incarcerated people of any country. Rehabilitation is not 100% effective, but it is effective most of the time. Those of us who have been convicted of sex crimes plead that you limit restrictions to those proven to be effective, and give us the opportunity to change.

Hanson's 2004 study includes the following recommendations

1. Given that the level of sexual recidivism is lower than commonly believed, discussions of the risk posed by sexual offenders should clearly differentiate between the high public concern about those offenses and the relatively low probability of sexual re-offense.
2. Within correctional literature it is well known that the most effective use of correctional resources targets truly high-risk offenders, and applies lower levels of resources to lower risk offenders.
3. Research has even suggested that offenders may actually be made worse by the imposition of higher levels of treatment and supervision than is warranted given their risk level.

Of course, increased resources could also be allocated towards treatment.

APPENDIX 2 – PORNOGRAPHY: A PUBLIC HEALTH ISSUE

Pornography has been around for centuries. Mt. Vesuvius erupted in 79 A.D., covering the city of Pompeii with volcanic ash and lava. When evacuations began in the 1700s, archeologists found not only beautiful villas, fountains, streets, and stores. They also found a surprising amount of phallic graffiti, as well as erotic murals in the ruins of brothels. Phallic imagery was common in ancient Greece and Rome; pornography is not a new invention.

The word pornography is derived from the Greek *porni*, meaning prostitute, and *graphein*, meaning to write. The Roman poet Ovid lived from 43 B.C. until 17 A.D., just one or two generations preceding Jesus Christ. His work *Ars Amaturia* (Art of Love) has been proposed as the first modern pornography. Pornography was not only a Western phenomenon. Child pornography has been around for centuries, long before scientists dreamed of the Internet. Early Arabic and ancient Greek literature speaks of sexual relationships between men and boys. Child pornography was also found in China as early as the 1400s, including in written stories about adults engaging in sex with children. Pornography became very popular in Japan during the early 1600s with new technologies of color woodblock printing. Modern Western pictorial pornography began during the 1800s with advances in printing technology. Henry Hayler of London was arrested in 1874 with approximately 130,000 child pornography images on photographic glass plates.

The mass popularity of pornography is more recent. Magazines like *Playboy* and *Hustler* became popular in the 1950s and 60s. Child pornography was sold illegally by mail and under the counter in some stores selling pornographic books and videos. However, the battle against child pornography seemed almost over. Federal efforts had virtually eliminated the availability of child pornography in bookstores and video stores. Postal inspectors had practically stopped the sending of child pornography through the mail.[xlv]

Then came the internet, with the "Triple A" engine noted by Dr. Al Cooper of being *a*nonymous, *a*ffordable, and *a*ccessible, which brought about a massive increase in the availability of child pornography.[xlvi] Engaging in internet pornography is convenient, immediate, stimulating, and disinhibiting.[xlvii] British scientist Susan Greenfield noted it is paradoxically isolationist while seemingly interactive if not intimate.[xlviii]

Most American and European countries permit pornographic images that would have been judged illegal forty to fifty years ago. We live in a culture that glorifies sex. All too often we are exposed to promiscuity, perversion, sadism, and brutality. Yet little thought may be given to the unintended consequences. We are expected to live as responsible, productive members of society and loving family members side by side with the proliferation of sexual images, which for many, trigger sexual addiction.

Sex is thought to be the third largest commercial sector on the internet (after software and computers), generating $2.5 billion annually.[xlix] More than a decade ago, Dr. Patrick Carnes estimated at least 100,000 sites prioritizing sexuality, with new ones being added every day. Dr. Gabriel Cavaglion [l]noted the variety of sexual activities available online, through pornographic picture libraries, videos and video clips, chat rooms, live strip shows, live sex shows, and voyeuristic webcam sites. These offer uninhibited excitement and distraction, as well as the promise and sometimes the inception of sexual affairs. Carnes estimated that 10% of adult internet users believe they are cybersex addicts.[li] In one study, Greenfield found that 60% of those seeking psychiatric treatment for problematic internet use were using the web to access sexually oriented material.[lii]

Most people are moderate users of the internet and do not experience problems with internet use. However, 4.7 million people visit pornography sites in excess of eleven hours per week. About 1% of users, mostly men, spend more than forty hours per week using the internet for online sexual activities.[liii] Researchers at Duquesne and Stanford Universities estimate that at least 200,000 Americans are addicted to e-porn.[liv]

Viewing internet pornography is primarily the habit of white, middle class and upper-class men with no criminal history – teachers and truck drivers, firemen and business leaders, lawyers and clergymen. Women in general are less visually aroused than men, but use of pornography by women is growing; 28% of pornography users are women.[lv] Among Christians, 47% admit pornography is a major problem in their homes.[lvi] Pornography reaches out to everyone. Nine out of ten children between the ages of eight and sixteen have viewed pornography on the Internet, often unintentionally.[lvii] Fifteen percent of adolescents have been exposed to child pornography.[lviii] In a report published by The Witherspoon Institute, Mary Eberstadt and Mary Anne Layden have noted the instant gratification of pornography. An unknown percentage of those exposed will develop a sexual addiction, potentially short-circuiting some important aspects of normal social and sexual development; the earlier the exposure the higher the likelihood of an addiction developing.[lix]

Pornography itself is protected by the Second Amendment. Only child pornography is clearly prohibited by law and universally condemned. The first reported FBI investigation of online child pornography was in 1993, when a dozen men were caught exchanging illegal images by email. Today child pornography ranks as a top law enforcement priority; even so, the number of online sexual offense cases that are prosecuted is still relatively small compared to the number of users.[lx]

Although many of those who view child pornography believe that they are committing a victimless crime, I learned that many of the children pictured relate being haunted by shame, embarrassment, and guilt throughout their lifetime. They worry that someone will recognize their image and attempt to contact them. Victims whose images are found online experience more depression and anxiety than other sexually abused children.[lxi] Those viewing child pornography and those supporting the industry need help to change their behavior and stop the damage.

Sexual addiction is a disease that brings harm to the addict and to others as well. Increasing our awareness of the potential harmful consequences of these practices could help us amend medical and mental health education, promote medical and scientific research, and influence public health policy. Cigarettes carry warnings from the Surgeon General of the United States; in contrast, internet pornography carries no such warnings. At the very least, public education and greater social discernment could ameliorate the damage from the sex and pornography industry.[lxii]

APPENDIX 3 – THE SCIENCE
OF SEXUAL ADDICTION

Living in the here and now, we are awash with sensations of the present, memories of the past, and fears for the future. Our actions are not determined by any one cause, they are the fulfillment of [multiple factors of] who we are at that particular moment.

– NATHANIAL PHILBROOK, *THE LAST STAND*.

Addiction, a Chronic Brain Disease

Although in treatment I dealt primarily with trauma and other psychological issues, and in recovery I dealt with spiritual issues, addiction also has genetic and physiological components. In this appendix I present a short summary of those issues.

Neurophysiology

"Addiction is about a lot more than behaving badly," says Dr. Michael M. Miller of the American Society of Addiction Medicine. Addiction hijacks key neuro-pathways of the brain – in particular, the motivational-reward pathway – leaving the individual vulnerable to obsessions and compulsions for engaging in destructive thoughts and impulses.

The average human brain contains 140 billion nerve cells, called neurons, which control our every thought and action. But the neurons don't touch each other. There is a small space between the neurons called a synapse. To communicate, the neurons release neurotransmitters into this space. Neurotransmitters are chemical agents within the synapse that pass electrical impulses from one neuron to the next. They are essential to the communication in our nervous system. There are over one hundred different known transmitter chemicals found in the brain, and more yet to be discovered. Abnormalities in the function of the neurotransmitter systems contribute to a wide range of neurological and psychiatric disorders that can lead to distortions in mood, thought, and behavior.[lxiii]

In 1956, James Olds discovered what we now call the pleasure center of the brain.[lxiv] He studied the effects of electrical stimulation on the brains of rats. When he stimulated certain areas with small amounts of electricity, the rats behaved as if they were experiencing pleasure. Scientists have traced a neurobiological track, now widely known as the motivational-reward pathway, that transmits pleasure from the ventral tegmental area of the midbrain, through the amygdala and the emotional processing center, to the nucleus accumbens in the forebrain.

Dopamine is thought to be a key neurotransmitter that conveys pleasurable sensations along this motivational-reward pathway. It gives us feelings of euphoria that come with many pleasurable activities, including engagement with drugs, alcohol, and gambling. Dopamine also contributes to the good feelings we get from engaging in sexual activity. It is a fundamental component in sexual motivation, carrying electrical impulses from one neuron to the next, helping us experience sex as pleasurable.

After the brain identifies something as pleasurable, another neurotransmitter, glutamate, allows us to remember the experience, along with any associated cues. Glutamate excites neurons from the forebrain back to the midbrain, transmitting a cognitive appreciation of the experience. Glutamate also lays down memories in the hippocampus, memories that serve as motivation to seek pleasure in the future, along with associated information to help us recreate it. Everything associated with sex – people, places, things, situations, and sensations – can become a cue to the brain, triggering sexual cravings.

In some people, unusually high amounts of dopamine may be released, alerting the brain that rewards are coming, and in response, an unusually large amount of glutamate is released, preparing the brain for the anticipated stimuli. Scientific evidence suggests that in advanced stages of an addictive process, neurotransmitters transmit and expand feelings of pleasure, encode memories that respond to triggers, and alter gene expression to enhance susceptibility to new cravings. These and other biological changes can last for years, even a lifetime, creating long-term vulnerability to addiction. [lxv]

Small differences in chemicals can generate significant differences in sexual experience and consequent behavior.[lxvi] The intensity of sexual motivation depends largely on the structure, function, and quantity of the chemicals within the brain and elsewhere in the body.

Genetics

Addiction runs in families. Most scientists believe that genetics account for about half the likelihood of an individual developing an addiction.[lxvii] Medical professionals are a long way from understanding all the genetic factors involved with addiction; but they have identified some of them and are in the process of identifying more.

In addition to these factors, before a person is born, genetics play a role. For example, one gene variation, D_2R_2, robs the reward center of dopamine receptors, lowering the level of this pleasure-producing neurotransmitter; some scientists hypothesize that the carrier of that variation is particularly motivated to escalate his or her sexual behaviors in order to experience a normal amount of pleasure.[lxviii]

Our cultural training tells us that monogamy is a decision. In 2008, however, a research team at Karolinska Institute in Sweden found that a section of a gene called RS_3 334 can come in variable numbers; a man might have no copies, one copy, or two copies. Further research showed that the number of copies correlated with the man's pair bonding behavior. Men with two copies were more likely to have marital problems.[lxix] The more copies of RS_3

334 the men had, the worse their marital problems. Also of interest, a study at Binghamton University in New York showed that young adults with a certain variation of the gene DRD (specifically the DRD_4 receptor gene DRD_4 VNTR), a gene that helps control dopamine release during sex, were more likely to report engagement in promiscuous behavior (e.g., "one-night stands") and engagement in adulterous affairs (e.g., "cheating") than those in the control groups.[lxx]

Adults with a particular set of genes are almost nine times more likely to commit a crime. Half of us have these genes. They are on the Y chromosome, which only men have. Men are much more likely to engage in deviant behavior than women. Note that the fact that not all men commit crimes is proof that genetics is not the only factor.[lxxi]

Most diseases are polygenetic, meaning that they result from contributions from multiple different genes.[lxxii] A series of interlinking interactions between organisms and the environment – "nature" and "nurture" – continue to shape the adult brain. Altered neurotransmitter activity can influence sexual disorders, and in the reverse, factors like stress, trauma, or repeated euphoric experiences can influence neurotransmitter activity and the expression of genes. Thus genetic inheritance is only the first step in complex developmental processes. The combination of our genetic makeup and our experiences determines how we develop. Some of us are resilient to stress, some are more vulnerable.[lxxiii]

APPENDIX 4 – REFLECTIONS ON SOCIETY: OVERREACTION, INJUSTICE, AND REHABILITATION

I PLANNED THIS BOOK TO be about sex addiction and recovery, and I believe the most important message I have is that a lot of sexual deviance is addictive behavior, and that sex addicts can and do recover and stop offending. I've tried to offer my own experiences, the verifiable experiences of others, and empirically sound data and information. In the course of my years of experience with sex addiction and recovery, including seven years in federal prison, I've developed some opinions I had not planned to include. Others have encouraged me to include them here. This appendix includes my viewpoints on some practices pertaining to sexual deviancy I perceive to be unjust or ineffective in our society.

Let me begin this section by being very clear: I was guilty of receipt and distribution of child pornography, and I pled guilty because I was guilty. I was doing things I knew were wrong and probably would have kept doing them had I not been arrested. I was addicted to child pornography, and my arrest began my process of recovery. I was not offered a plea bargain; I pled guilty without one. I was treated fairly by the investigating agents, the prosecutor, and the judge. My attorney charged me a fair price, advised me well, and represented me superbly. I am grateful to all of them. Ninety-seven months seemed like a long sentence, but it was less than half the sentence many others have received for similar offences. I have no complaints about how my case was handled, and am not lobbying for any personal gain.

How Sex Offenses Are Viewed by the Public

Society establishes behavioral expectations that are not to be violated. Some are simple, like not jaywalking or not talking too loudly at a funeral. These generally carry minor penalties or are completely ignored. Others, like terrorist activity, murder, or child sex abuse, may bring lengthy prison sentences or death. Sex offenses reach into some of our most basic fears. Many people have done things they wish they could take back, or of which they are deeply ashamed, but even relatively minor sexual violations such as hiring a prostitute or indecent exposure may bring general censure, ridicule, and punishment. Participants may be labeled immoral, sinful, sick, or perverted.

When a person has been arrested one time for a sex offense, that offense is considered to define his entire character. Many people automatically assume that a person who has committed one sex offense is likely to commit another one; a man who exposes himself is thought likely to also be a rapist; a man who looks at child pornography is considered likely to molest a child. It does not matter if he has completed treatment, regularly attends church and twelve-step meetings, and has never committed a single other offense. His overall worth as a human being is judged by much of the public by that single event.

The public takes a very dim view of sexual deviance. No one would disagree that sexual abuse of children is intolerable and that those who sexually abuse children should be punished. But sex offenses against children have become a national obsession and the pursuit of sex offenders a witch hunt. Someone accused is considered guilty before the facts are released, and even if acquitted he will carry the stigma of being an accused child molester for the rest of his life.

In the November 26, 2012 edition of *Sports Illustrated*, Phil Taylor wrote about a football coach accused of a sexual offense. This was not Jerry Sandusky, who had been found guilty of abusing boys while coaching at Penn State, but rather a coach at Minnesota State–Mankato, who recorded two short videos on his cellphone of his three young children getting out of a bubble bath. His children, ages five, eight, and nine, asked him to film them performing a skit. They were naked. The video was discovered when he sent the phone in for repairs. Coach Todd Hoffner was put on paid leave and was allowed no contact with his team. Four days later he was arrested on felony child pornography charges and taken to jail, where he spent the night. His reputation has been damaged beyond repair. The coach had no history of inappropriate conduct and no child pornography was found on his home computer. The Human Services Department found no reason to separate the coach from his children. An aggressive prosecutor saw "lewd exhibition of the genitals." Hoffner's friends say the prosecutor is the only one who sees anything pornographic in the videos.

The story doesn't end there. Three months later, in November 2012, a judge dismissed the charges. But the nightmare continued. In December, Hoffner was suspended for twenty days, reassigned to an administrative job, and in May was fired for "undisclosed reasons." Hoffner, who knew his photographing his children was innocent, wanted not only to be exonerated of criminal charges, but vindicated by the university as well.

In April 2014, twenty months after his arrest, an arbitrator ruled in Hoffner's favor. He had been wrongly terminated and must have his old job back if he wanted it, and was to be repaid the salary he lost with interest. Hoffner had roots in Mankato and decided to return to his old job. On Wednesday, April 16, Hoffner returned to the practice field, along with Athletic Director Kevin Buisman, the same man who had escorted him off the field twenty months before. But the nightmare was still not over. The players refused to practice.

Todd Hoffner had led his team to a very successful 34-13 record during the four years he had coached at Minnesota State-Mankato. But during the two seasons Hoffner had been gone the team went 22-2 under interim coach Aaron Keen, losing only in the NCAA Division II tournament. The players said they preferred Coach Keen. After a two-hour closed-door meeting the following day, the players agreed to return to practice. Coach Keen returned to his former position as offensive coordinator. The 2014 team, again under Todd Hoffner's leadership, went 14-1, losing only the national championship game.[lxxiv] Although the criminal charges against Hoffner were dismissed and he has been returned to his job, he and his family suffered twenty months of personal nightmare because he dared to take a short video of his naked children performing a skit. To some he will always be remembered as the coach who produced child pornography.

In their eagerness to catch those who are predatory against children, many in society have developed a public and prosecutorial presumption of guilt of the accused that conflicts with the principle of presumed innocence. Innocent people's lives are destroyed by a single accusation.

Prominent individuals found guilty of predatory sexual behavior present an opportunity to educate the public. Those who are sexually addicted are sick people, not bad people, and society would do well to consider their actions disease-driven, deserving of compassion, rather than immoral, deserving of shame.

Many Sentences are Neither Reasonable nor Fair

Not all people caught in a rush to judgment are innocent, but real justice demands that everyone be treated reasonably and fairly. Guilt and punishment is determined by facts and law, but the results are not always fair, and they often damage lives unnecessarily. The following are some examples.

Fetishes are hard to understand by those of us who do not have them. Webster defines a fetish as an object or body part whose real or fantasized presence is psychologically necessary for sexual gratification. Barry served on his community's school board and was a union leader in the plant where he worked. Barry had a diaper fetish. He downloaded and exchanged videos of children and adults being diapered or wearing diapers and masturbated while watching them. Was this a harmless diversion or a federal crime? The prosecutor told Barry he was afraid of what he *might* do. Barry was sentenced to 10 ½ years in federal prison for receipt and distribution of child pornography.

Phil was the head of the English Department at a large Eastern university. He and his wife were unable to have children, but both became sexually aroused by pictures of small, naked children and looked at those pictures, which he downloaded from the Internet, while engaging in intercourse. Arrested for possession of child pornography, Phil defended himself by showing that he could legally purchase books with similar pictures at the university bookstore. He was convicted of possession of child pornography and served five years in federal prison.

Retired from the Air Force, Marshall lived with four women. The police found child pornography in their home on a computer that belonged to one of the women. The prosecutor claimed that the pornography belonged to Marshall because "Women wouldn't do that." Marshall denied knowing that the pornography was even on the computer, pled not guilty, and went to trial. Several of the women testified in Marshall's defense. Two FBI agents claimed that Marshall had verbally admitted the pornography was his. Despite Marshall's denials and the lack of any physical proof, Marshall was convicted and sentenced to ten years in federal prison.

George was a prominent man. He had served in the House of Representatives of his Western state and was a successful businessman. Arrested for the possession of child pornography that he had downloaded from the internet, George's case, like mine, received a significant amount of media coverage. George admitted his guilt, and his attorney expected him to receive a sentence of five-to-seven years. A few days before sentencing the judge received an email from a young man claiming George had abused him as a child years before. The young man agreed to testify at George's sentencing.

George had evidence that he was living in another country at the time the young man claimed to have been abused. The young man did not appear at the sentencing, so George could not present his evidence and his attorney could not cross-examine the young man, but the judge had read the email and interviewed the young man on the telephone. George was sentenced to 17 ½ years in prison, ten years above the federal guidelines. George's appeal of his sentence was not successful. The right to cross examine-witnesses at trial is guaranteed; the right to cross-examine witnesses at sentencing is not.

Law Enforcement Tempts and Entraps Men to Commit Crimes

On Dateline NBC's *To Catch a Predator,* a top-rated television program for several years, millions of viewers watched pathetic men, invited on the internet to have sex with a fifteen- year- old girl, show up to be arrested for soliciting a minor who did not exist. The public found this entertaining. The targets of the sting will spend years in prison. In a similar situation, Les, whom I knew in prison, was a depressed twenty-nine-year-old socially inept young man who had never had a date. Excited by a fifteen-year-old girl he had met in an internet chat room, he went to her home after she expressed a desire to have intercourse with him. His "date" was a police officer. Les claimed in court that he had been entrapped, lied to, and lured into a place he would not otherwise have gone. He was sentenced to 10 ½ years in federal prison.

Barry Glassner, in his book *The Culture of Fear* (1999), writes about the negative aspects of the nationwide fear of internet pedophiles.[lxxv] There are surprisingly few cases of people being attacked by people who locate them online. The internet is described as a "city with no cops." Yet since 1993, the FBI has conducted an operation called "Innocent Images" in which agents post seductive messages on the internet, attempting to lure child predators into responding to their provocative messages. Normally they end up arresting lonely and harmless men who have never touched a child but find themselves unable to resist "sex4u," who is dreaming of kinky sex. Our courts continue to rule that these intervention strategies are not illegal entrapment or an invasion of privacy.

Glassner quotes David L. Sobel, an attorney with the Electronic Privacy Information Center, asking, "Are we making the world a better place by tempting some of these people to commit crimes they may not have otherwise committed?" I have met over one hundred inmates imprisoned for viewing, distributing, or transporting child pornography or soliciting a minor on the internet. Only one was also convicted of seducing a child. Juan, a shy twenty-year-old college student from Texas, met and "fell in love with" a fifteen-year-old girl from another state. He flew to her home city, dated her, and engaged in what he mistakenly believed was consensual sexual activity (although, of course, the girl was too young to consent to sexual relations with an adult). Caught in the act by her father, Juan was arrested and sentenced to ten years in federal prison. In Juan's case, the government will spend more than $300,000 in imprisonment costs alone, not counting the significant costs of investigation, prosecution, eventual supervised release, and a lifetime on the sex offender list. What have we accomplished, beyond warehousing a young man who made a mistake and making him almost unemployable? Of course, his conduct was unacceptable. But isn't there a better way to handle it?

Overreaction is Causing Unjust Treatment

Some treatment professionals and defense lawyers say that the concentration on pornography has become excessive. Many of those caught never intended to hurt a child. Defense attorney Peter Greenspun said, "Sending people to prison for five or ten or fifteen years for looking at pictures is like killing an ant with a sledge hammer."[lxxvi] Congress demands long, harsh sentences. First-time offenders with no previous criminal record convicted of looking at and trading pictures they neither took nor purchased are often sentenced to twenty years in federal prison. The cost to the taxpayer for incarceration alone is $600,000 for a twenty-year sentence, as measured in today's dollars.

There is enormous and unfair disparity between federal and state sentences for internet sex offenders. Because most child pornography is seen online, pornography offenses are often heard in federal courts. Federal sentences for first-time offenders convicted of exchanging pornographic child images call for a minimum of five years and a maximum of twenty. Barry was sentenced to 10 ½ years for exchanging pictures of children being diapered. Phil received a five-year sentence for looking at Internet pictures of small children, pictures he could have legally purchased in a bookstore.

The difference between the length of prison sentences for sex crimes in federal courts and in the courts in most states is significant. Sentences in most states are considerably less. A former Aspen, Colorado, high school drama teacher was sentenced to eighteen months in jail when images of young girls were found on his home computer. A Massachusetts masseur was sentenced to up to three years in prison for secretly videotaping himself sexually assaulting at least fifteen clients. Families of federal inmates are angered by the disparity.

Sentences for soliciting a minor online handed down in federal courts average almost ten years. Gene's sentence for inviting a fifteen-year-old girl (in reality an FBI agent) to come to his small town was 9 ½ years. Les went to trial, was found guilty, and was sentenced to 10 ½ years – an additional year for exercising his constitutional right to trial.

What happens to those convicted in state courts of soliciting a minor? Brian was caught in a police sting in Texas trying to arrange sex with a fifteen-year-old girl on the internet. He was sentenced to ten years deferred adjudication, a type of probation that means he will not be convicted of a crime if he fulfills the court's requirements for ten years, nor will he spend a single day in prison.[lxxvii] A former University of New Hampshire professor was sentenced to one year in jail and five years probation for soliciting someone he thought was a fourteen-year-old girl, actually a police officer. Clearly the disparity between these sentences in state courts and federal sentences is considerable.

Twenty-year-old Juan received a ten-year federal sentence for engaging in intercourse with a fifteen-year-old girlfriend he met online. What happens in state courts to those convicted of similar offenses? Former football player Lawrence Taylor pled guilty to two charges of sex with a sixteen-year-old. He was sentenced to six years probation. A former Alamorado (New Mexico) High School coach pled guilty to entering the home of a seventeen-year-old student through an unlocked window and forcibly touching her, earning himself a one-year sentence. A former county and state corrections officer in Nebraska was given four-to-five years in prison for molesting a twelve-year-old girl over the course of a year. These are all serious crimes, but Congress, responding to unrealistic public fear, has overruled recommendations from the Federal Sentencing Commission by legislating unnecessary and unrealistically high sentences.

Sentences in neighboring Canada are also much lower. A Toronto-area computer expert was sentenced to twenty-one months for operating an internet server with some 2,500 transactions exchanging child pornography. A U.S. missionary, caught with nearly 5,000 illegal images, received a twenty-month penalty, one of the longest child pornography sentences in Manitoba history.

Federal Judges are Rebelling

In the past decade changes to sentencing laws have effectively quadrupled the average prison term for collectors of child pornography from twenty-one months to ninety-one months.[lxxviii] These acts are disgusting to most people, but not everyone accepts the idea that they warrant twenty years or more in prison. In possession cases where there is no evidence the defendants sought to abuse minors, some judges are giving much lower sentences than the guidelines recommend. U.S. District Judge Robert W. Pratt gave a seven-year sentence to one defendant, even though the guidelines called for eighteen-years. He said the sentencing guidelines for child pornography crimes "do not appear to be based on any sort of (science) and the court has been unable to locate any particular rationale for them beyond general revulsion that is associated with child exploitation-related offenses".[lxxix]

Judge William Griesback sentenced a defendant to five years in prison instead of the recommended eight. He wrote, "The fact that a person was stimulated by digital depictions of child pornography does not mean he has or will in the future seek to assault a child." Troy Stabenow, a public defender whose critique of child pornography sentences has been cited by judges, noted, "You shouldn't punish someone for something they haven't done—it's not American".[lxxx] He added, "The recent sentences are signaling...that judges across the country think the current system is broken."

Federal Judge Jack B. Weinstein has come to be identified for combating "the unnecessary cruelty of the law." Judge Weinstein has challenged the strict punishment and attacked the mandatory five-year minimum sentence faced by those who receive child pornography. He recently stated that he doesn't approve of child pornography, but he does not believe that individuals who view the images, but do not produce it or see the children, present a threat to children. "We are destroying lives unnecessarily," he said. "At most they should be receiving treatment and supervision." Douglas Berman, a professor at Ohio State University's Moritz College of Law, studies sentencing issues. He says, "What has caused concern in courts across the nation is that we have a lot of relatively law-abiding individuals sitting in the basement downloading the wrong kind of dirty pictures facing not just prison sentences, but incredibly long prison sentences".[lxxxi]

U.S. District Judge William Sessions, the chairman of the sentencing commission, says judges have been nearly unanimous that the guidelines and mandatory minimums restrict their ability to sentence defendants based on the specifics of each case and the particular defendant. Perhaps change is coming.

Release from Prison Does Not End Punishment
Society has a right and an obligation to guard against reoffending by those convicted of sex crimes. But after release many sex offenders suffer again from unnecessary rejection based on groundless fears. Fear overwhelms compassion. The point of laws requiring disclosure of the offender's place of residence, employment, and education was to protect the public, and particularly minors, from *violent* sex offenders. The vast majority of individuals convicted of sex offenses are not violent offenders. Fewer than 3% of all sex offenses are rape-murders and sadistic assaults.[lxxxii] All convicted sex offenders are placed on state and federal sex offender registries – rapists and child molesters, along with those who possess child pornography. But also on the lists are eighteen-year-olds who slept with their sixteen-year-old girlfriend or those convicted of indecent exposure. In some states registration and notification laws are applied to youth, resulting in children being labeled as sex offenders for life. Children as young as ten years old are found on some state registries.[lxxxiii]

In an effort to treat all sex offenders equally, fairness has gone out the window. Those convicted of statutory rape, a contact offense, are considered among the most dangerous offenders, the same as predatory rapists. No differentiation is made, even though rape is a violent offense. In Texas, someone arrested twice for urinating in public is considered a Tier 1 sex offender, the most dangerous level.[lxxxiv]

Approximately 800,000 sex offenders have been placed on state and federal registries. Some would make good neighbors. Some are dangerous. Law enforcement agencies in some locations have been overwhelmed. On September 3, 2009, the *Wall Street Journal* reported:

> The case of Phillip Garrido, who allegedly held Jaycee Dugard in his back yard for 18 years despite monthly law enforcement visits, is forcing California officials to acknowledge a fundamental problem with that state's sex offender registry. The list keeps expanding, while the numbers of officials who monitor sex offenders grow at a much slower rate.[lxxxv]

Vast resources are spent monitoring nonviolent offenders rather than keeping close track of the more dangerous offenders.

Some restrictions are nationally legislated, others drawn by states or communities. In many communities, sex offenders may not live or go near schools, parks, or other places children gather. The distance varies – 1 mile, 2,500 feet, 1,000 feet, 500 feet. Some communities don't allow sex offenders at all. A July 6, 2009, *Fort Worth Star Telegram* editorial notes that "experts have seen little correlation between where the sex offenders live and where they commit their crime."[lxxxvi]

Still, the wife of an offender, an exhibitionist about to be released from prison, lived at the very edge of her community's "no live" zone. She asked the city council for an exception, which was granted. Her husband's probation officer would not approve. He was held in state prison until his wife found a home for them in another county.

On completing his sentence, Evan, a mentally ill offender who served 6 ½ years for possessing less than two hundred images of naked teenage girls that he had found on the internet, was released from federal prison to the state where he committed his crime, not the state where his family lived. There was not a single halfway house in that state that accepted sex offenders, so he was released to a work release program in a county jail. When he could not pay

$51 for the psychiatric medication he had been provided, the county refused to let him leave the jail. For months, he was confined to a county jail because of a $51 bill for medication, even though he had completed his prison sentence. If he could have been released, he may have been able to earn the money to pay for his medication.

When has a sex offender paid the debt he owes to society? Not when his time in prison has ended, nor when his probation has been completed. Additional limits and disclosures are placed on sex offenders. Their picture may be placed on the internet, postcards sent to people living within 1,500 feet (or more) of their residence, and their conviction noted on their driver's license. Registration laws not only affect sex offenders, but their families as well. Rand, who was sent to prison for emailing a pornographic image to a minor he didn't know was a minor, lived with his elderly parents between the time he was arrested and incarcerated. By the time Halloween came, Rand was already in prison. Although Rand no longer lived there, the police came to his parents' house with a sign: "Do not stop for candy. A dangerous sexual predator lives here." His mother, who had taught Sunday school for forty years, was required to put the sign in her yard, even though her son was in prison.

Some Regulations are Counterproductive

It's an advantage to everyone for convicted felons to find a job, support their families, pay their fines, complete their education, and find decent housing. Current laws make this very difficult. Ex-felons find it 50% more difficult to find a job than non-felons. Former sex offenders find it 50% more difficult than other felons. In some states the name and location of a former offender's employment is placed on Internet registries, discouraging employers from hiring them.

Many of the regulations that have serious unintended consequences have been shown to provide no protection for the public. Because of the severity of sex offender registration and notification laws, some family members, psychologists, social workers, or those charged with protecting children are reluctant to report sex abusers. Because of the difficulties created by unnecessary laws, 100,000 sex offenders have disappeared, failed to register, and gone into hiding. These are the offenders we should worry about. Sex offenders who have family support, who have jobs, and who are established in the community, register and follow the rules no matter how difficult. Those who can't and won't follow the rules, those who tend to be the more dangerous ones, disappear and are unsupervised.

Other Penalties Would Be More Effective

We know that those engaging in addictive deviant behavior can be helped by psychological treatment. Yet fear deters people from seeking treatment. State and federal laws require the reporting of child abuse or possession of child pornography, in some cases requiring reporting even by therapists in whom the patient confides or clergy to whom he confesses. Some men who have molested a child do seek help for the child and themselves, even though they know that they will be punished severely for what they did. Others do not, deterred by the fear of punishment. Some, addicted to child pornography, do not get help because of the fear of severe consequences. A woman said to a friend, "My husband is looking at child pornography and won't stop. What should I do?" The answer that her friend would like to give is to insist that he get some help. But when attempting to get help results in five or ten or fifteen years in prison, the decision becomes more difficult. Is it possible that strict reporting requirements result in less reporting, and consequently the abuse of more children?

Evan (the young man who was later released to a county jail work release program) was twenty-five years old. Homeless and mentally ill, he helped at an Internet café in a small town in North Dakota and slept on the café owner's couch. The café owner recognized that Evan was looking at pictures of teenage girls on the computer. He called the police to get Evan some help. But Evan didn't get help; he was simply locked in a county jail, placed in a pod with seven other inmates. One of them asked Evan why he was in jail, and Evan told him. Another inmate pulled Evan from his top bunk, slammed him onto the concrete floor, and beat him into a coma. Evan came out of the coma in the local hospital eighteen days later and eventually was released from the hospital. Suicidal, he checked himself into the state mental hospital, where his mental condition was stabilized. He was finally getting the help he needed. Four months later the FBI picked him up at the hospital. They had found 167 pictures of naked teenage girls on the computer Evan was using, pictures he had downloaded from the Internet. None of the girls were engaged in sexual activity. He was convicted of possession of child pornography and sentenced to 6 ½ years in federal prison. The cost of keeping an inmate in federal prison is about $30,000 per year. What was the cost of the help Evan really needed?

Robert Freeman-Longo reports, "The best way to stop sexual abuse is to prevent it before it begins…When laws result in a decrease in the reporting of a particular crime, increased plea bargaining, and causing harm to innocent people, they cannot be seen as preventive".[lxxxvii] Recall Dr. R. Karl Hanson's meta-analysis that showed that 90% of convicted sex offenders who completed treatment did not reoffend. Offenders who have not been caught are afraid to turn themselves in to get help because they could be subject to severe punishment. **Treating men who have offended, or those inclined to offend, as early as possible is much less costly than incarceration and would likely increase the number of men who seek help and in the long run reduce the number of victims.** Freeman-Longo adds that registration and notification laws have "done little to protect people and prevent crimes." At the time of his report there was little or no evidence that these laws had any impact on reducing childhood sex abuse.

Writer Luke Malone wrote about Adam, a sixteen-year-old pedophile.[lxxxviii] Adam had discovered images of preteen girls and boys on the internet and quickly realized that he found the images arousing. Not only was he sexually attracted to young children, he was particularly attracted to children who were visibly being abused. He was terrified. At age sixteen, he recognized that he was a pedophile, just like the man abusing those small children, and he didn't want to hurt anyone. Where could he get help?

Malone writes, "Most pedophiles first recognize an attraction to children when they themselves are between 11 and 16, mirroring that of any other sexual awakening." They did not seek their sexual orientation to small children; their orientation found them. Adam writes, "I know that pedophiles don't chose to be pedophiles. I didn't want my attraction. I don't want my attraction. But the attraction is there, and all I can do is try to curb it?" Where do these children get help?

Today it is very difficult for someone who has pedophilic urges and hasn't acted on them to get help. In contrast to the more than 17,000 treatment facilities in the United States that address drug and alcohol problems, we have about 150 programs dedicated to treating process addictions—88 for eating disorders, 30 for compulsive gambling, 25 for sexual addiction, and 10 for internet addictions, and none dedicated to pedophilia.[lxxxix] The paucity of treatment programs for these addictions reflects remissness to this emerging field by mental health practitioners, most of whom have had no formal training for addressing these problems.[xc] Sexual addiction is not even a diagnosis recognized in the current Diagnostic and Statistical Manual of the American Psychiatric Association.[xci]

Those who have acted on their pedophilic urges face even more difficult decisions. Mandatory reporting laws make getting help more difficult. Although Adam had not molested a child, he had been viewing child pornography. In many states Adam would be subject to mandatory reporting. Psychologists and other mental health professionals would be afraid to *not* report him, even if they are not required to, because if Adam did later molest a child the therapist could be subject to civil and criminal penalties, in addition to jeopardizing his or her license to continue to practice and being additionally disciplined by his or her professional institution.

After a great deal of frustration because of his failure to find help, Adam started a private online chat group for teenaged pedophiles who had not molested a child but did look at child pornography. That takes a lot of initiative for a teenager. Shouldn't these children be able to get good professional help without subjecting themselves to arrest?

There is no coherent theory of criminal punishment and treatment for nonviolent sex offenders at the federal or state level. N.W. Galbreath writes:

> We need to distinguish between non-ill, dangerous individuals who have a malicious disregard for laws and the well-being of others, and those decent, struggling individuals who are much in need of therapeutic assistance.[xcii]

Other experts are concerned that long-term imprisonment is detrimental to the offender. Psychologist and researcher Michael Seto writes:

> Ideally, the prospect of ... criminal justice sanctions would act as a deterrent and reduce recidivism. Unfortunately, the evidence is clear that criminal sanctions do not reduce recidivism; in fact (they) increase the risk of recidivism... Criminal sanctions still serve the important purposes of offering justice for victims, signaling society's moral opprobrium toward the behavior, and incapacitation for a period of time for those individuals who pose an unacceptable risk to public safety...long sentences are best reserved for high risk offenders.[xciii]

Barry Glassner noted that we waste tens of billions of dollars and manpower on largely mythical problems by putting people in prison cells who pose little or no danger to others, and on programs designed to protect young people from dangers few of them will ever face. Public concern that sex offenders are forever unable to control their behavior and routinely reoffend flies in the face of facts. Isn't it time to resolve the simultaneous and conflicting interests of people with compulsive sexual disorders and those who want to be protected from them?[xciv]

Whatever the psychological reality might be, civilizations have to act as if the individual is responsible for what the individual does. Whether a person is responsible for his actions determines the way we punish. An individual convicted of accidental manslaughter is punished less severely than a person convicted of murder in a fit of passion, which is punished less severely than an individual who committed a planned murder. If a person's act was due to a neurological process over which the individual had little control, doesn't that mitigate, but not excuse, the guilt?

Sentences should be proportional to the harm done. Those who directly abuse children or those who produce child pornography should receive the most severe sentences. Those who actively engage in the selling of child pornography should still receive a more severe sentence than those who simply look at the images because they create a market for the pornography. Those who simply possess child pornography should receive less severe sentences.[xcv]

As of 2008, the United States had 2.3 million people behind bars, leading the world by far in the percentage of its citizens in prison. Most of those in prison are there because of an addiction to alcohol, drugs, sex, or gambling, diseases that can be treated. Certainly, society benefits from incarcerating violent and repeat offenders, but years of punishment and the debilitating effects that go with it have little to do with correction or rehabilitation. Many of those behind bars could be dealt with in a more effective manner than imprisonment.

We want to believe that incarceration and supervision following release from prison deter further criminal behavior. Imprisonment provides solace to victims and families, signifies society's disapproval of the behavior, and keeps dangerous people locked up. However, there is clear evidence that not only does incarceration not reduce criminal behavior, but harsher sentencing results in loss of family contact and employment, and thus actually increases the likelihood of repeat criminal behavior.

Michael Seto notes that public education campaigns about online sexual offending tend to focus on the danger posed by online predators who target young children, lie about their interests, and use personal information to target victims. Research simply does not support those assumptions. These campaigns would be more effective if they focused on vulnerable teenagers rather than young children, highlighted the reasons youth should not engage in sex with adults, and taught them how to respond to inappropriate online requests.[xcvi]

Seto continues to explain that the fact that these claims are made and are not upheld in research strongly supports the need for changes in policy and practice. Money spent on campaigns warning youths about the dangers of communicating with strangers online is not available to use for more effective communication programs. Dollars spent requiring long prison sentences for first-time online child pornography offenders are not available for effective treatment programs. A long sentence for those whose only offense is viewing child pornography keeps those individuals from participating in the lives of their families and from contributing financially. Seto states, "If we, as a society, are going to make these choices, then we should strive to make them fairly and effectively in the light of the scientific knowledge we have about online sexual offending." He adds that we should use the information gained from risk assessment research to guide our interventions, both in targeting higher risk individuals and in identifying potential sex offenders for treatment or supervision.[xcvii]

Forward-looking risk assessments of future criminal activity have been deemphasized in favor of backward-looking procedures designed to place the blame for past conduct. **We know that treatment for sex addiction works.** Wouldn't we be better off with mandated treatment for first-time nonviolent offenders, or short "shock sentences" combined with treatment?

True justice is not about punishment; it's about restoration and rehabilitation. America can do better.

APPENDIX 5 – TWELVE STEP RESOURCES FOR SEX ADDICTION AND CODEPENDENCE

COSA
For men and women who have been affected by someone else's compulsive sexual behavior
9219 Katy Freeway, Suite 212, Houston, TX 77024
866-899-COSA (2672)
info@cosa-recovery.org
www.cosa-recovery.org

Co-Dependents Anonymous (CoDA)
P. O. Box 33577
Phoenix, AZ 85067-3577
info@coda.org
www.coda.org

Recovering Couples Anonymous
For couples recovering from addiction
P. O. Box 11029, Oakland, CA 94661
1-877-663-2317
info@recovering-couples.org
www.recovering–couples.org

S-Anon
For those who have been affected by sexual addiction in a relative or friend
P. O. Box 17294, Nashville, TN 37217
800-210-8141
sanon@sanon.org
www.sanon.org

Sex Addicts Anonymous
For those seeking recovery from sex addiction
P. O. Box 70949, Houston, TX 77270
800-477-8191
info@saa-recovery.org
www.saa-recovery.org

Sexaholics Anonymous
For those seeking recovery from sex addiction
P. O. Box 3565, Brentwood, TN 37024-3565
866-424-8777
saico@sa.org
www.sa.org

Sex and Love Addicts Anonymous
For those seeking recovery from sex and love addiction
1550 NE Loop 410, Suite 118, San Antonio, TX 78209
210-828-7900
www.slaafws.org

Sexual Compulsives Anonymous
For those seeking recovery from compulsive sexual behavior
P. O. Box 1585, Old Chelsea Station, New York, NY 10013
1-800-977-HEAL (4325)
www.sca-recovery.org

ACKNOWLEDGEMENTS

I OWE A HUGE DEBT of gratitude to a multitude of men and women who assisted me in this effort.

First, I give deep thanks to my wife and family for their support through my addiction, incarceration, and recovery. Most families do not survive intact through an ordeal like ours. Each of you is a hero to me.

Almost all the cases cited in this book came from a personal relationship with the individuals involved. You were generous in allowing me to enter your lives in the most personal way. Most were brave enough to allow me to use your name, although I chose to not do so. You have my deepest gratitude.

To Dr. Charles S., my prison roommate for several years, I offer my most sincere thanks. You shared your extensive medical knowledge and kept me honest. You would not allow me to jump to conclusions that were beyond what the evidence supported. I'm sure I did so anyway, but that's my fault, not yours. I could not have done this without you.

To Wally and Simon and others who volunteer to come into our prisons and help those in sincere need. You know who you are. You are appreciated.

To those who shared in my recovery at twelve-step meetings, I appreciate your patience and unstinting support. Those of you I met before my incarceration guided me into recovery. Those courageous men who faced incredible personal risk by admitting to your faults while in prison supported me through a deeply difficult time. I left prison with confidence you would be there for me also, and you were. No one recovers alone, and I could not recover without you.

To the therapists, treatment professionals, and clergy who have shared your wisdom and guidance, thank you.

In the course of writing this book, many men and women have read all or parts of it and offered advice. Jason and Lee developed my web page. Jesse painted the front cover art. Your many suggestions made this book better.

To each of the authors of works listed in the bibliography, your writing and research strengthened my understanding. I have plundered your ideas mightily. The conclusions, however, are my own. Any errors are solely mine.

ENDNOTES

Introduction
i. 2 The book *Alcoholics Anonymous,* which provides the basis for all twelve-step programs, was written in 1939. All quotations from the book *Alcoholics Anonymous* come from the fourth edition, published in 2001. In the future it will be identified in the endnotes as *AA*.

ii. 2 *AA* pages 83-84.

iii. 2 AA page 563

iv. Bradshaw, J. (1988/ 2005). *Healing the Shame that Binds You.* Deerfield Beach, FL: Health Communications, Inc.

Chapter 5 – Trauma
v. Finkelhor's 1984 book, *Child Sexual Abuse: New theory and research,* related groundbreaking information in the area of child sexual abuse. See page 189.

vi. Pia Mellody, *The Intimacy Factor, 1903*

Chapter 14 – Into Treatment
vii. This concept is supported by Korshak, Nickow, and Straus in their 2014 book *A Group Therapist's Guide to Process Addictions.* I use this reference many times.

viii. From an article "Is Everything Addictive?" by V. Fahey, page 27 of the January-February 1990 edition of *Health*.

ix. Galbreath, N. W. (2002). Paraphilias and the Internet. In A. Cooper, *Sex and the Internet: A Guidebook for Clinicians* (pp. 187-205). Philadelphia: Brunner-Routledge.

x. Berlin, F., & Krout, E. (1994). *Pedophilia: Diagnostic Concepts, Treatment, and Ethical Considerations*. Retreived from http://www.bishop-accountability.org.

xi. Grov, C., Parsons, J., & Bimbi, D. (2010). Sexual compulsivity and sexual risk in gay and bisexual men. *Archives of Sexual Behavior*, 39, pp 940-949.

xii. Carnes, P. (2001). *Out of the Shadows, Third Edition*. Center City, MN: Hazelden.

Chapter 15 – Understanding Sexual Addiction

xiii. Korshak, Nickow, & Straus. (2014). *Introduction to process addictions for group psychotherapists*. New York: American Group Psychotherapy Association.

xiv. Ibid.

Chapter 16 – What! You too? I Thought I Was the Only One

xv. Dayton, T. (2000). Trauma and addiction. *Health Communications*, xvi-xvii. Page 5

xvi. Parnell, L. (2007). *A Therapists Guide to EMDR: Tools and Techniques for Successful Treatment*. W.W.Norton & Co.

xvii. Mellody, P., Miller, A. W., & Miller, J. K. (2003). *Facing Codependence*. New York: Harper Collins. Pp 7-44.

xviii. AA page 63.

Chapter 17 – I'm Not Much, But I'm All I Think About
  xix. Eagleman, D. (2011). *Incognito: The Secret Lives of the Brain.* New York: Pantheon Books. Pg. 145.

Chapter 18 – Family Therapy
  xx. *Sexaholics Anonymous.* (1989). SA Literature.

Chapter 19 – Learning About Recovery
  xxi. Shaw, B. R. (2005). *Addiction and recovery for dummies.* Hoboken, NJ: Wiley Publishing.

  xxii. Korshak, Nickow, & Straus. (2014). *Introduction to process addictions for group psychotherapists.* New York: American Group Psychotherapy Association.

  xxiii. Some experts, including some courts, question the reliability of the plethysmograph, and others have concerns about the implications on civil liberty for those required to participate.

  xxiv. Korshak, Nickow, & Straus. (2014). *Introduction to process addictions for group psychotherapists.* New York: American Group Psychotherapy Association.

  xxv. Slutske, W. S. (2006). Natural recovery and treatment-seeking in pathological gambling: Results of two U. S. national surveys. *American Journal of Psychiatry,* 163, 297-302.

xxvi. Kapleau, P. (1989/1965). *The three pillars of zen: Teaching, practice and enlightenment.* New York: Doubleday.

xxvii. Korshak, Nickow, & Straus. (2014). *Introduction to process addictions for group psychotherapists.* New York: American Group Psychotherapy Association.

Chapter 25 – Recovery and the Twelve Steps

xxviii. Korshak, Nickow, & Straus. (2014). *Introduction to process addictions for group psychotherapists.* New York: American Group Psychotherapy Association.

xxix. AA pp. 96-97

Chapter 26 – Going Home

xxx. Jimenez, J. R. (1957/1985). *Platero and I.* Austin: University of Texas Press, translated by Eloise Roach.

xxxi. All Bible quotes are from the *NIV Study Bible.* (1995). Grand Rapids: Zondervan.

xxxii. AA page 164

xxxiii. Palmer, T. (2005). Children who are subjects of abusive images. In E. Quayle, & M. Taylor, *Viewing Child Pornography on the Internet.* Dorset, England: Russell House Publishing.

Chapter 27 – Spirituality

xxxiv. AA, p.417

xxxv. Frankl, V. (1959). *Man's Search for Meaning*. New York: Simon & Schuster, Inc.

Appendix 1 – Does Treatment Work

xxxvi. Berlin, F. (1991). Media Distortion of the Public's Perception of Recidivism and Psychiatric Rehabilitation. *American Journal of Psychiatry, November 1991*, 1572-1576.

xxxvii. Barlow, D. H., & Durand, V. M. (2009). *Abnormal Psychology, An Integrative Approach*. Belmont, CA: Wadsworth Cengage Learning, pp. 379-381.

xxxviii. Ibid, p. 381.

xxxix. Lee, C. (1911, December 5). This Man is Addicted to Sex. *Newsweek*, pp. 48-50.

xl. Hanson, R. K. (2004). *Predictors of Sexual recidivism: An Updated Meta-Analysis*. Public Works and Government Services Canada, and Hanson, R. K. (2006). Sex Offender Recidivism. *National Associations of Sentencing Commissions*, (p. Power Point Presentation). Philadelphia.

xli. Hanson, R. K. (2004). *Predictors of Sexual Recidivism: An Updated Meta-Analysis*. Public Works and Government Services Canada.

xlii. Harris, A., & Hanson, R. K. (2004). *Sex Offender Recidivism: A Simple Question*. Public Safety and Emergency Preparedness Canada.

xliii. Hanson, R. K. (2002). First report of the Collaborative Outcome Data Project on the effectiveness of psychological treatment for sex offenders. *Sexual Abuse: A Journal of Research and Treatment*, (14(2), 169-194.

xliv. Hanson, R. K. (2004). *Predictors of Sexual recidivism: An Updated Meta-Analysis.* Public Works and Government Services Canada.

Appendix 2 – Pornography: A Public Health Issue

xlv. Galbreath, N. W. (2002). Paraphilias and the Internet. In A. Cooper, *Sex and the Internet: A Guidebook for Clinicians* (pp. 187-205). Philadelphia: Brunner-Routledge.

xlvi. Cooper, A. (1998). Sexuality and the internet: Surfing into the new millenium. *CyberPsychology & Behavior*, 1, 187-193.

xlvii. Korshak, Nickow, & Straus. (2014). *Introduction to process addictions for group psychotherapists.* New York: American Group Psychotherapy Association.

xlviii. Greenfield, S. (2004). *Tomorrow's people: How 21st century technology is changing the way we think and feel.* London: Penguin Books.

xlix. Carnes, P. (2007). *In the Shadows of the Net.* Center City, MN: Hazelden.

l. Cavaglion, G. (2009). Cyberporn dependence:Voices of distress in an Italian internet self-help community. *International Journal of Mental Health and Addiction*, 7(2), 295-310.

li. Carnes, P. (2007). *In the Shadows of the Net.* Center City, Minnesota: Hazelden.

lii. Greenfield, S. (2004). *Tomorrow's people: How 21st century technology is changing the way we think and feel.* London: Penguin Books.

liii. Ross, M. W. (2002). Men Who Have Sex with Men and the Internet: Emerging Clinical Issues and Their Management. In A. Cooper, *Sex and the Internet* (pp. 47-69). New York: Brunner-Routlege.

liv. MSNBC. (2000, January 26). Stanford/Duquesne Study. *Washington Times.*

lv. Family Safe Media. (2006). *Pornography Statistics.* Retrieved from Family Safe Media: http://www.familysafemedia.com/pornography_statistics.html

lvi. *Internet Program Review.* (2003). Retrieved from Program Statistics.

lvii. London School of Economics. (2012, January) downloaded from http://majorchange.org.

lviii. Sabina, W. et. al. (2008). The Nature and Dynamics of Internet Pornography Exposure for Youth Under 18. *Cyberpsychology and Behavior, 11,* 691-93.

lix. Eberstadt, M. et. al. (2010). *The social costs of pornography: A statement of findings and recommendations.* New York: Witherspoon Institute.

lx. Seto, M. C. (2008). *Pedophilia and Sexual Offending Against Children.* Washington DC: American Psychological Association.

lxi. Palmer, T. (2005). Children who are subjects of abusive images. In E. Quayle, & M. Taylor, *Viewing Child Pornography on the Internet*. Dorset, England: Russell House Publishing.

lxii. Sussman, S. L. (2011). Prevalence of addictions. A problem of the majority or the minority? *Evaluation and the Health Professions*, 34 (1), 3-56.

Appendix 3 – The Science of Sexual Addiction
lxiii. Purves, D. (2011). *Neuroscience, 5th Edition*. Sinauer Associates.

lxiv. Olds, J. (1956). Pleasure centers in the brain. *Scientific American, 195*, pp. 105-116.

lxv. McCauley, K. T. (2012). *Pleasure Unwoven: A Personal Journey About Addiction, a study guide to the film*. Salt Lake City: Institute for Addiction Study, pg. 30.

lxvi. Purves, D. (2011). *Neuroscience, 5th Edition*. Sinauer Associates.

lxvii. ASAM, A. S. (2011). *Public Policy Statement: Defination of Addiction (Long Version)*. Chevy Chase, MD: American Society of Addiction Medicine.

lxviii. Ratey, J. (2008). *Spark*. New York, NY: Little Brown and Company.

lxix. Walum, H., Westerg, L., & et.al. (2008). Genetic variation in the vasopressin receptor 1a gene (AVPR1A) associates with pair-bonding behavior in humans. *PNAS*, September 16, vol. 105, no. 37, 14153-14156.

lxx. Garcia, J. E. (2010). Associations between dopamine D4 receptor gene variation with both infidelity and sexual promiscuity. *PLoS ONE (5) 11*, 1-6.

lxxi. Eagleman, D. (2011). *Incognito: The Secret Lives of the Brain*. New York: Pantheon Books. Pg. 159.

lxxii. Ibid. Pg. 210.

lxxiii. McCauley, K. T. (2012). *Pleasure Unwoven: A Personal Journey About Addiction, a study guide to the film*. Salt Lake City: Institute for Addiction Study, pg. 32.

Appendix 4 – Reflections on Society: Overreaction, Injustice, and Rehabilitation

lxxiv. This information was taken from the following three articles: Taylor, P. (2012, November 26). All It Takes To Create a Monster. *Sports Illustrated*, p. 68.; Gregory, S. (2014, April 21). *A Coach is Cleared of Child Porn Charges, but His Ordeal Drags On*. Retrieved from time.com: http://time.com/70230/todd-hoffner-minnesota-state-mankato/; Associated Press. (2014, April 17). *foxnews.com*. Retrieved from sports: http://foxnews.com/2014/04/17/minnesota-state-players-will-play-for-coach-exonerated-of- child-porn-charges.

lxxv. Glassner, B. (1999). *The Culture of Fear*. New York: Basic Books.

lxxvi. Markon, J. (2007, December 16). *Washington Post*.

lxxvii. Carlton, J. (2008, March 8). *Associated Press*, Registered sex offender hopes voters judge content of his 'current character' lxxviii. Sulzberger, A. (2010, May 21). Defiant Judge Takes on Child Pornography Law. *New York Times; NYtimes.com.*

lxxix. Efrati, A. (2008, October 23). Making Punishments Fit the Most Offensive Crimes. *Wall Street Journal*, p. A14.

lxxx. Ibid.

lxxxi. Sulzberger, A. (2010, May 21). Defiant Judge Takes on Child Pornography Law. *New York Times; NYtimes.com*

lxxxii. Freeman-Longo, R. E. (2001). *Revisiting Megan's Law and Sex Offender Registration: Prevention or Problem.*

lxxxiii. Ibid.

lxxxiv. Fort Worth Star Telegram. (2008, March 31). Criminal Justice, A Safer Texas. *Fort Worth Star Telegram*, p. 12B.

lxxxv. Knutson, R., & Scheck, J. (2009, September 3). Sex Registry Flaws Stand Out. *Wall Street Journal.*

lxxxvi. Fort Worth Star Telegram. (2009, July 6). Sex Offender Bans, Worth Thinking Through. *Fort Worth Star Telegram.*

lxxxvii. Freeman-Longo, R. E. (2001). *Revisiting Megan's Law and Sex Offender Registration: Prevention or Problem*, p. 7-8.

lxxxviii. Malone, L. (2014, August 10). *You're 16. You're a Pedophile. You Don't Want to Hurt Anyone. What Do You Do Now?* Retrieved from medium.com/matter: https://medium.com/matter/youre-16-youre-a-pedophile-you-dont-want-to-hurt-anyone-what-do-you-do-now-e11ce4b88bdb#.t3ea535si lxxxix. These numbers are now increasing, but the number of treatment centers from process addictions is limited and usually very expensive. The numbers in the text are from Hagedorn, B. (2009). The call for a new diagnostic and statistical manual for mental disorders diagnosis: Addictive disorders. *Journal of Addictions and Offender Counselling*, April, 20(2), 110-127.

xc. Freimuth, M. S. (2008). Expanding the scope of dual diagnosis and co-addictions: Behavioral addictions. *Journal of Groups in Addiction and Recovery*, 3 (3-4), 137-160. Korshak, Nickow, & Straus. (2014). *Introduction to process addictions for group psychotherapists.* New York: American Group Psychotherapy Association.

xci. American Psychiatric Association. (2013). *Diagnostic and Statistical Manual of Mental Disorders, Fifth Edition.* Arlington, VA: American Psychiatric Association.

xcii. Galbreath, N. W. (2002). Paraphilias and the Internet. In A. Cooper, *Sex and the Internet: A Guidebook for Clinicians* (pp. 187-205). Philadelphia: Brunner-Routledge.

xciii. Seto, M. C. (2013). *Internet Sex Offenders.* Washington, DC: American Psychological Association.

xciv. Glassner, B. (1999). *The Culture of Fear.* New York: Basic Books.

xcv. Seto, M. C. (2013). *Internet Sex Offenders.* Washington, DC: American Psychological Association.

xcvi. Ibid.

xcvii. Ibid.

ABOUT THE AUTHOR

BRADY C. WAS AN INTERNATIONALLY recognized expert in the field of education, as well as a married man with three grown children. Unknown to everyone, he was also a sex addict who spent his spare time viewing child pornography on the Internet. After his arrest and imprisonment, he began a long road back with the help of therapy and twelve-step programs. *Walking through the Storm: A Story of Recovery from Sex Addiction* is both a cautionary tale and an inspirational example to other addicts and their families.

Made in United States
Troutdale, OR
12/07/2023